Sledgehammer

Women's Imprisonment at the Millennium

Pat Carlen

Professor of Sociology
Department of Social and Policy Studies
Bath University

First published 1998 by
MACMILLAN PRESS LTD
Houndmills, Basingstoke, Hampshire RG21 6XS
and London
Companies and representatives
throughout the world

ISBN 0–333–74083–1 hardcover
ISBN 0–333–74606–6 paperback

A catalogue record for this book is available
from the British Library.

This book is printed on paper suitable for recycling and
made from fully managed and sustained forest sources.

10   9   8   7   6   5   4   3   2   1
07   06   05   04   03   02   01   00   99   98

Printed and bound in Great Britain by
Antony Rowe Ltd, Chippenham, Wiltshire

For
Chris Tchaikovsky
Founder of the campaigning group
Women in Prison

Contents

Preface

1997 It is a sad fact that the particular requirements
of women in prison have been overlooked in study
after study into conditions in prison (Sir David
Ramsbotham, HM Chief Inspector of Prisons, 1997 in
Home Office 1997b)

Not so. During the last two decades of the twentieth century all
the extreme and discriminatory conditions in which women
prisoners in Britain were being held (and, at the time of going
to press, still are being held), and which the Chief Inspector
highlighted in his 1997 *Thematic Report* (HM Chief Inspector of
Prisons 1997b), had already been documented in study upon
study conducted by women researchers and campaigning
groups. And they had all been just as studiously ignored by the
Prison Service and its political masters.

Yet, it is not appropriate to blame the Prison Service. For,
however many official reports and critical books are written,
what can the Prison Service do when it is charged with containing so many women for whom prison – any prison – is totally
inappropriate? Or when, as happened during the early 1990s, a
Home Secretary prioritizes prison security above all other
considerations, including those of common humanity, common
sense and common decency? In such circumstances, it creates a
sledgehammer – a penal instrument which smashes at the
already-smashed and which, in its penal ferocity, is a disgrace to
a civilized society.

Sledgehammer is the title of this book and it is intended to be
suggestive of a threefold argument, that

**women's imprisonment in England and Wales at the
end of the twentieth century is: excessively punitive;
totally inappropriate to the needs of the women being
sent to prison; and ripe for abolition in its present
form.**

But, although the book focuses primarily on conditions in the
women's prisons in the 1990s, it also contends that it is no

longer plausible, acceptable or useful to go on blaming the Prison Service for all of the sledgehammer's crudities and absurdities. A more effective approach towards women's imprisonment would set in motion a holistic strategy to ensure that the size of the female prison population is drastically reduced in the future. For the sad fact of the matter is that, despite the steady accumulation of research and official reports in the last couple of decades, women's imprisonment (under which term I include the related processes of custodial sentencing and penal confinement) is shot through with as many (constantly changing) absurdities and inhumanities as it ever has been.

As I write this in early 1998, I have before me the latest in a long line of critical reports, the excellent *Thematic Review of Women's* Prisons (HM Chief Inspector of Prisons 1997b), a detailed investigation undertaken by the Chief Inspector after he walked out of London's Holloway Prison in disgust at the gaol's dirty physical condition in December 1995. It is a thorough, well-researched report, a welcome and comprehensive source of up-to-date and important statistical data. However, most of the information contained therein was already known and was repeatedly brought to the attention of the appropriate authorities in the months immediately prior to the 1995 inspection. Some of the conclusions (such as the call for yet more research *and* more prisons for women) are hardly radical. The whole question of whether too many women are being sent to prison was beyond the Inquiry's remit.

But does it really matter *what* the Review recommended? Will any of the recommendations be acted upon?

Not if the lack of response to previous reports is anything to go by.

So, why another book?

Sledgehammer is primarily a sociological study of women's imprisonment in England at the end of the twentieth century. It is also written, in part, as a polemic. For I, like many others, am puzzled to know what more can be done to provoke the changes required if women's imprisonment in England is, in the twenty-first century, to cease being the scandal that it is in the twentieth. Very little has come of the long line of inquiries which, though they always imply that 'something *will* be done' about the state of the women's prisons, perennially add 'but not yet'. Not until we have had 'more research' or 'a further inquiry'.

Overwhelming evidence of the mismatch between the present state of the women's prisons and the needs of the women who are currently being sent to them is already available in the reports of a variety of inquiries held in the last fifteen years. A main task of this book is to show why the lack of a holistic response to women offenders has continued to perpetuate a system that, despite some minor attempts at reform, and the humane concerns of the people working in the women's gaols, is still quite over the top in the punishment it inflicts on women who have committed relatively minor or first-time crimes.

In 1993, before his Party came to power, the present Prime Minister said of the Prison Service,

> What we require is not a series of policy initiatives that are reflex responses to particular events in our Society, but a thought-out policy, a strategy if you like, that deals with all the various aspects of the problems that we face and doesn't attempt to isolate the Prison Service from the rest of the Criminal Justice System. (Blair 1993:127)

To no part of the penal process is that exhortation more applicable than to the processing of women in the criminal justice system. On the evidence that is before them at the end of 1997 there should be sufficient horror at conditions in the women's prisons to prompt the present government to act in support of the type of holistic policy which the Prime Minister recommended when he was in opposition.

ACTION NOW is required to ensure that a more holistic, less destructive and more civilized policy on the treatment of women in the criminal justice system is actually devised and implemented.

Pat Carlen, January 1998

1990s Statistical Profile of Women's Imprisonment

- Between December 1992 and December 1995 the number of women prisoners rose by 57 per cent from 1353 to 2125 (Penal Affairs Consortium 1996:2)
- Around 40 per cent of women in prison (excluding foreign nationals) are likely to have been in local authority care at some time before the age of 18
- On 30 June 1996 a total of 355 females (20 per cent of the total sentenced female population) were serving custodial sentences for violence against the person as compared with 9230 males (22 per cent of the total sentenced male population) serving sentences for the same type of offence. Another 1926 males were serving immediate custodial sentences for rape (Home Office 1997b)
- In a study of 200 female prisoners in 1993 it was found that the women were 'broadly typical ... of female prisoners elsewhere. They were generally young, criminally unsophisticated, and were mainly in prison for property offences. Over 40 per cent were mothers of dependent children and nearly a half of these mothers were single parents. [N]early half the women reported having been physically abused and nearly one third reported having been sexually abused. (Morris *et al.* 1995 in Prison Reform Trust 1996)
- In 1996 16 per cent (314) of female British nationals in prison were from non-white ethnic minority groups; while a further 318 women (ie approximately 14 per cent of the total female prison population) were foreign nationals (Home Office 1997b:10)

Acknowledgements

Many people have given me a great deal of help with this book. But I should say straightaway that, although the carefully expressed and thoughtful contributions of the prison staff who were interviewed inspired many of the arguments put forward in the following pages, I know that my overall interpretations of their accounts, and the conclusions then drawn from them, are not ones with which all (or maybe any!) of them will agree.

Nonetheless, I wish first to acknowledge with gratitude and respect the assistance given to me by many prison personnel. I promised all of them that I would protect their anonymity, and for that reason they shall remain nameless here. But they know who they are, and to all of them, a very big 'thank you'.

As always, I wish to pay grateful and respectful tribute to the hundreds of women prisoners and ex-prisoners who, over the last twenty-five years, have not only given me information, but who have also explained to me and then discussed, some of the finer points of prisoner politics.

Thanks also go to: the Nuffield Foundation which provided a Small Grant for travel to interviews and for tape transcription; and the University of Bath which granted four months' research leave while the book was being written.

At NACRO'S Women Prisoners' Resource Centre I was helped by Jackie Lowthian, Florence and Stacey; at 'Women in Prison' by Maggie Hall and Liz Dewsbury; at Kelly House by Eileen O'Sullivan; at Keele University by Anne Worrall; in Australia by Kerry Carrington; in New Zealand by Kit Carson; and at the Home Office's Prison Research Unit by Sarah Jones. Each, at some stage of the research, 'opened doors' that would otherwise have remained firmly closed.

Lesley Bailey transcribed the interview tapes with her usual efficiency. I was especially grateful for her good humour and comradely cheer while she was engaged in the task.

The contribution of former Home Secretary, Michael Howard, will be apparent throughout the book: his innovative reign at the Home Office seems to have inspired several of the prison staff interviewed to comment on his 'penal reforms' with a vehemence and analytic insight (and also in a language!) which made their interview-transcripts a joy to read.

My greatest thanks go to Chris Tchaikovsky who has selflessly given of her time, contacts and expertise both to me and countless other researchers into women's imprisonment during the fourteen years since she founded the campaigning Group 'Women in Prison'. I dedicate this book to her with gratitude, admiration and affection.

Pat Carlen, Central London, January 1998

Introduction

1996   I've seen the way young girls get manhandled. Arms
twisted up behind their backs, heads pushed nearly
between their legs. It's distressing. It's horrible.
(Jill, prisoner in Holloway, 1996. Aged 45)

1997   A woman prisoner was forced to undress and
undergo an intimate internal examination while
handcuffed to an escorting officer, according to a
complaint upheld by the prison ombudsman. The
report, completed last year but not previously
released, reveals that although the woman 'practically begged' for her handcuffs to be removed, they
were kept on throughout. 'I was in a lot of embarrassment' the prisoner told the ombudsman. 'As I
took off my knickers, it was like the officer had physically undressed me herself. Everywhere my hand
went, her hand went too.' ... The woman, who
underwent a rectal examination because she was
suffering a stomach complaint, told the ombudsman: 'I was in stress, pain and very uncomfortable.
My hands were shackled above my head with two
officers looking on'. (The *Guardian*, 4 April 1997)

In January 1996, Channel 4 News secretly filmed a female prisoner while she was in labour in a London hospital. When the
film was shown there was public uproar, not because the woman
had been transferred to an outside hospital to give birth, (her
crime had been the non-violent one of stealing a handbag), but
because the film provided incontrovertible evidence that in the
last decade of the twentieth century women prisoners were
being manacled to *any* prison officer – whether female or male –
detailed to guard them during labour.

After much prevarication the prisons' minister at the Home
Office admitted that the manacling of women in labour had
been going on for several months – the manacles not being
removed until the actual birth had commenced.

Once more women's imprisonment was under the spotlight, and once more all the old questions were being raised: Is it necessary to send so many women to prison? Are women treated differently to men by the police, the courts and the prisons? Why are so many poor, black and mentally ill women in prison? And so on. But, for the women who had been campaigning for better conditions in the women's prisons for well over a decade, the main question was: What have we achieved? Because, for many of us, the most depressing (though not the most shocking) prison news that winter had been in December 1995 when the Prison Inspectorate had withdrawn from an inspection visit to Holloway Prison because it was in too filthy a state to be inspected. Here it was – officially confirmed – that after years of being the focus of a vigorous campaign for better conditions, ten years after its rebuilding had been completed, and towards the end of the twentieth century, London's one and only prison for women was infested with rats and cockroaches! Even a prison officer breached the profession's usual media reticence to speak to a journalist about the appalling conditions in Holloway for both inmates and staff.

> There are cockroaches everywhere. You hear them crawling about at night ... I've often seen the rats ... It's like going down a tunnel to the Middle Ages. (Prison Officer on the conditions in Holloway Prison. The *Guardian* 20 December 1995)

In 1983 I wrote a book about Cornton Vale, Scotland's only prison for women, situated just outside Stirling (Carlen 1983). I did the research and wrote the book as a 'one off', and did not expect to do any more prison research in the future, let alone another book on *women's* imprisonment. What changed my mind was a meeting later in 1983 with an ex-prisoner, Chris Tchaikowsky, the founder of the campaigning group Women in Prison, who, after reading *Women's Imprisonment*, invited me to join the group of (mainly) ex-prisoners she was then trying to get together to campaign on behalf of women still inside. The initial task was to raise public awareness of Britain's invisible women prisoners – via vigils outside Holloway Prison, letters to the newspapers, magazine articles, and, eventually, lobbying and books. It was with these activities that Women in Prison (WIP) was born.

The first literary campaigning endeavour of WIP's founder members was the production of a book, *Criminal Women* (Carlen *et al.* 1985), which comprised four autobiographical accounts of women's crimes and women's imprisonment. The account of Josie O'Dwyer's time in prison in the 1970s (O'Dwyer and Carlen 1985) was so convincing in all its harrowing detail that it was subsequently reprinted several times (Open University 1989; Giddens 1992 and 1997; Polity 1994; Priestley 1995). Other books and reports which documented the state of the women's prisons during the the 1980s were McShane 1980; Peckham 1985; Dobash, Dobash and Gutteridge 1986 ; Seear and Player 1986; Mandaraka-Sheppard 1986; Bardsley 1987; and Padell and Stevenson 1988.

Between 1983 and 1989 women's imprisonment was always in the news. We therefore became hopeful that the extensive publicity might soon begin to bear fruit in terms of fewer women being sent to prison and better facilities and less repressive regimes being provided for those few who were. In 1989 a small grant from the Nuffield Foundation enabled me to investigate the current situation of women offenders either vulnerable to, or actually receiving, a sentence of imprisonment. The results of those investigations were published as *Alternatives To Women's Imprisonment* (Carlen 1990), a book whose title was indicative of its optimism.

On the face of it, 1989 appeared to be a propitious moment for assessing whether there were indeed grounds for optimism about the Home Office's 1970 prediction that, 'as the end of the century draws nearer, penological progress will result in ever fewer or no women at all going to prison' (Home Office 1970). Home Office officials had recently and successfully challenged the government's policy of penal retributivism with the Green Paper Punishment, Custody and the Community (Home Office 1988; Rutherford 1996), and the Probation Service had been charged with preparing tough and effective community alternatives to imprisonment for all offenders convicted of less serious crimes. Many senior members of the Probation Service saw the new policies as being of especial importance to women, and were looking forward to shaping non-custodial programmes which might lead to a decrease in the size of the female prison population (cf NAPO 1988:18). The National Association for the Care and Resettlement of Offenders (NACRO) set out a very positive and imaginative agenda entitled *A Fresh Start for Women Prisoners* (NACRO 1991).

There was also a slight loosening-up of regimes in the women's prisons, as more outside groups offering services to women prisoners were allowed into the establishments, and a greater emphasis was placed on 'throughcare' and the special medical needs of inmates. Although there was still much to be done to reduce the female prison population and remedy the inequities and poor facilities suffered by women in prison, there was also a pervasive optimism amongst those involved in innovative non-custodial and prison projects that things could only get better. That optimism was misplaced.

Even while probation services were drawing up plans for new non-custodial programmes of supervision, a tougher welfare climate was already threatening young people's ability to survive increasing unemployment and homelessness, and was undermining, too, the best attempts of the probation and social services to keep vulnerable young people out of trouble. Young mothers living alone with their babies were beginning to be portrayed as representing a new threat both to family life and to the welfare economy, while the young people themselves painted a different picture – of unemployment, destitution, and a despair about ever being able to secure a decent wage. The government's determination to minimalize the role of the welfare state was resulting in savage cuts in benefits and these punitive measures were falling most heavily upon women and young (especially black) people who, for one reason or another, were already suffering extremes of poverty (see Byrne 1987; Bull and Wilding 1983; Glendinning and Millar 1988, 1992). Moreover, though the Tory governments had backed detailed schemes purportedly designed to save money by reducing the prison population, they had, at the same time, counterproductively indulged in a scaremongering rhetoric about a 'breakdown in law and order' so as to divert attention from the failure of their economic, health and education policies. Such reckless and contradictory tactics, (together with the sentencing and penal confusion they caused), played a major part in creating a New Punitiveness, primarily directed towards young people in general, but also towards young, single mothers in particular. This New Punitiveness had several interrelated dimensions, but the three that have most affected women in the criminal justice and penal systems are: 'The New Politics of Community Penality'; 'The New Folk Devils' (ie 'single mothers' and 'unattached male youth'); and 'The Fetishism of Prison Security'.

THE NEW POLITICS OF COMMUNITY PENALITY

[The Women in Prison Group has always argued that because so few women in prison have committed serious crimes of violence] the female prison population might safely be much reduced; even to the point where it could be seen as the first step in a more general prison abolitionism (Carlen 1990). But in 1988 the policy document, *Punishment, Custody and the Community* (Home Office 1988) proclaimed that the government of the day also wanted to see a reduction in the prison population. Unsurprisingly, theirs was neither an abolitionist programme, nor even a straightforwardly reductionist policy; it was state transcarceralism. In other words, it was a policy designed to bring the pains of imprisonment into the 'community' by ensuring that non-custodial penalties were made so punitive that sentencers would have more confidence in awarding them. Concomitantly, more and more people (eg women at home whose errant sons and husbands would be placed under curfew) would perforce have their homes turned into outposts of the prison estate (cf Aungles 1994; Fishman 1990).

And 1992 did indeed see an overall decline in the prison population. However, 'by the early spring of 1993 it was clear that a number of countervailing forces were gaining ground rapidly' (Rutherford 1996:127). Almost before the Criminal Justice Act 1991 was on the statute book, magistrates, judges, police and media were clamouring against what was rather prematurely portrayed as a 'new leniency'. Vigilante groups were formed and applauded for patrolling the parts that the official police no longer seemed able to reach, and the government set about fashioning new and more punitive legislation (see Criminal Justice Act 1994, which abolished the 'right to silence' of suspects and introduced new punitive measures against squatters and travellers).

The new Home Secretary, Michael Howard, soon made clear his own position on penal policy. In a speech to the annual conference of the Conservative party in 1993, he declaimed:

Prison works. It ensures that we are protected from murderers, muggers and rapists – and it will make many who are tempted to commit crimes think twice. (Rutherford 1996:128)

The new Director of Prisons, Derek Lewis, was quick to support Mr Howard in his attempts to make prisons more unpleasant than they already were (Lewis 1997).

THE NEW FOLK DEVILS

It was in the period 1988–94, during the time that three consecutive Conservative Home Secretaries were attempting to remodel penal administration in three fundamentally different ways (prison reductionism – Douglas Hurd; prison privatization – Kenneth Clarke; and security fetishism – Michael Howard) that two new sets of folk devils appeared: 'unattached youth' – quickly to become the butts of all kinds of penal fantasies – from hard labour for ten-year-olds, to bringing back both corporal and capital punishments; and relatedly, 'single mothers' – to be 'deterred' from the single state by punitive changes in welfare and housing legislation.

The 1990s attack on single mothers in Britain was provoked by the stew of anti-poor prejudices that comprise right-wing versions of underclass theory. Basically, the rhetoric went like this: that, found in neighbourhoods containing high numbers of fatherless families headed by never-married mothers, 'underclass' poor are those who, having been reared by permissive mothers and a supportive welfare state, now refuse to work and, instead, engage in predatory, violent and society-threatening crime (Murray 1990:1994). Implicit in the theory was the old notion that all crime is explicable in terms of family structure and parenting, together with the even older calumny that women are the roots of all evil. (As Helena Kennedy's excellent 1992 book title puts it, 'Eve Was Framed'!). It was undoubtedly some such atavistic conception of women's place that was responsible for the Conservative Government's threat in the mid-1990s to bring in punitive legislation to deter single women unsupported by males from bearing children. As a host of studies had already suggested that sentencers were prejudiced against single women rearing children without men (Worrall 1981; Carlen 1983; Farrington and Morris 1983; Dominelli 1984), it was likely that this generalized punitiveness towards single mothers (Dennis and Erdos 1992) would have further malign influence on their passage through the criminal justice and penal systems (Edwards 1984; Eaton 1986; Worrall 1990).

THE FETISHISM OF PRISON SECURITY

Whatever influence the New Punitiveness towards single mothers may or may not have had on the sentencing of female offenders, the dimension of the 'New Punitiveness' which had the greatest impact on the women's prisons in the 1990s was the fetishism of prison security (in terms of both the prevention of escapes and the crackdown on illicit drugs) which followed in the wake of the Woodcock Inquiry (Home Office 1994), the Learmont Review of Prison Service Security (Home Office 1995b) and the introduction of Mandatory Drug Testing (MDT).

Descriptions of the effects that both the Learmont Inquiry Report and MDT have had on women prisoners' regimes will feature prominently in later chapters of the book. However, it was as a result of the ways in which both Woodcock's and Learmont's recommendations plus MDT were being implemented in the women's prisons that, during 1995 and 1996, the stories of the new degradations and pains to which women prisoners were being subjected came thick and fast. There were lurid stories about Holloway's new Dedicated Search Teams (dressed in tracksuits and baseball caps) making women submit to the most intimate and intimidating strip searches; and about Mandatory Drug Testing in some of the women's gaols not only requiring women to urinate in front of two female officers, but in requiring them to do so with their hands held up well above their heads.

> Women strip-searched by jail heavy-mob... . Women in Holloway prison are being subjected to an intensified and intimate form of strip-search by officers apparently looking for drugs, writes Lucy Johnston. In the past month, at least four women in the north London jail claim they have been made to bend over, spreadeagled and naked, while officers carry out vaginal inspections. The officers are believed to be part of a search team dubbed the 'squat team' or heavy mob' by inmates, introduced after the Whitemoor escape in 1994.

Inmates describe the team as an intimidating group dressed in black PVC leggings, Dr Martens boots and baseball caps. (*The Observer*, 24 November 1996)

And in 1985 we had thought that things could not get worse! Remembering my own injunction at the end of *Women's Imprisonment*, that 'while prisons exist we should never presume that we always already know what goes on behind the walls', (Carlen 1983:218), I decided to make yet another investigation into the meanings of women's imprisonment. This book is the outcome. Yet, though what follows is not an 'official' history of women's imprisonment at the end of the twentieth century, I did have a great deal of help from all those governors, prison officers and others working in the women's prisons who, to summarize a dominant view, thought that it was time that they should 'tell it like it is from the staff point of view'.

In fact, what distinguishes this book from others written about women's imprisonment in the last twenty years is that some of the most critical voices to be heard in it are those of the officers, governors, nurses, teachers and probation officers who work in the women's prisons, and who are at last speaking out about some of the penal absurdities and degradations that they were forced either to witness or be party to during the 1980s and 1990s, when the politico-penal screw was tightened on male and female prisoners alike, and male and female prison staff too.

SOURCES OF INFORMATION

Most of the ideas put forward in the following pages have been developed over the fifteen years since I wrote *Women's Imprisonment*, and they draw on knowledge gained in three subsequent research studies, countless discussions with prison staff and ex-prisoners, and innumerable visits to women's prisons both at home and abroad. However, in view of the steep increase in the numbers of women being sent to prison in Britain in the 1990s and the many changes occurring in the prisons during the same period, I thought that in order to make an up-to-date assessment of women's imprisonment at the end of the twentieth century, I should conduct a small-scale project especially to investigate the ways in which those population rises and regime innovations were affecting the women's gaols.

Between December 1996 and October 1997 I visited 12 (of the 16) penal establishments for women – nine 'closed' and three 'open'. Seven governor grade staff, 24 prison officers (17 female and 7 male), 31 prisoners, four probation officers, two education officers, one psychologist, and one member of a Board of Visitors were interviewed during those visits. In addition I interviewed eight recently-released female ex-prisoners, two members of a different Board of Visitors, one ex-governor of a women's prison, three workers from NACRO's Women Prisoners' Resource Centre, three workers from Women in Prison's Holloway Remand Project, the Director of Women in Prison, one senior official at Prison Service Headquarters, and one senior official in the Home Office. Quotations from all interviews have either been anonymized or (in the case of women prisoners – except Lindis Percy) pseudonymized. As a result of these additional interviews I was able to interview prisoners who had recently been in Brockhill and Cookham Wood, two of the prisons that I was unable to visit. At the time of writing I had been given no first-hand accounts of either Highpoint or Foston Hall prisons, both of which had only been recently opened. Several of the prisoners interviewed made reference to time served in HM Prison and Remand Centre Pucklechurch which had closed during the previous year.

Of the total of 39 prisoners and recently-released prisoners interviewed, six were from ethnic minority groups in Britain, two were black foreign nationals and one was a white foreign national. Twenty of the 39 women had lost their accommodation when they had come into prison. Eight of the 36 British nationals had spent some part of their childhoods in local authority care.

All of the women interviewed in prison had been selected, and then invited to volunteer, by prison officers. Except in one prison at the end of the research, where I especially asked that younger women be approached, I asked officers to select prisoners whom they considered to be 'typical, average' prisoners. This was to help avoid any suggestion at a later date that my information had come primarily from 'troublemakers' or 'disturbed people'. Of the ex-prisoners that I interviewed outside prison, four had been approached by hostel or project workers, and three of the other four had wanted me to interview them because they had very specific grievances to air in relation to the establishments in which they had served their sentences.

THE BOOK'S OVERALL ARGUMENTS AND CONCLUSIONS

1. Women's imprisonment at the end of the twentieth century incorporates and amplifies all the anti-social modes of control that oppress women outside prison, and it does so primarily because a coherent and holistic policy on women's imprisonment has never been developed.

2. A coherent and effective policy towards women in the criminal justice and penal systems will only be developed when it is recognized: that women's crimes are committed in different circumstances to men's; that women's lawbreaking is, on the whole, qualitatively different to men's; and that therefore the response to both men and women lawbreakers should be in part gender-specific rather than merely crime and sentence specific.

3. The main components necessary to the development of an holistic policy towards women's imprisonment from outside the prison system would be: a Ministry of Social and Criminal Justice to co-ordinate all aspects of social policy in relation to social exclusion, including the monitoring of social exclusion via potentially anti-social modes of punishment such as prison regimes falling below minimum standards of decency and humanity; a Sentencing Council to monitor and regulate the sentencing of women offenders; and a Women's Prisons' Unit to monitor regimes in the women's prisons.

4. All proposed prison regime innovations should be gender-tested and ethnicity-tested to assess their potential for differential impact on prisoners according to gender and/or ethnic minority affiliation.

5. Different regimes for men and women (or differential modes of rule implementation) can be justified on the principle of *ameliorative justice* – a principle that assumes that as women (and black women in particular), because of their different social roles and relationships and other cultural

difference, are likely either to suffer more pains of imprisonment than men, or to suffer in different ways, the prison
authorities are justified in running different regimes for
women to make up for (or ameliorate) the differential pains
of imprisonment attributable to gender or ethnic difference.

6. There are three possible futures for women's imprisonment
    – regressive, reformist and reductionist. If women's prisons
    are not to get worse, a principled approach combining
    reform and reduction must be adopted. If nothing is done,
    the women's prisons will undoubtedly deteriorate still
    further. If there is merely piecemeal reform the women's
    prison sector will remain in its usual pendulum state of
    reform and regression. Only a principled reform pro-
    gramme, combined with a commitment both to holism and
    reductionism is likely to avoid the regressive tendencies to
    which prisons (especially at times of political and economic
    conservatism and the heightened social anxieties associated
    with rapid social change) are prone.

7. The Prison Service should no longer bear the major portion
    of blame for the state of the women's prisons. All the requi-
    site materials for transforming the traditional forms of
    women's imprisonment into a much more rarely-used and
    (less wasteful) women's penal confinement are already
    available in the skills, commitment and creativity of the
    many good staff working in the Prison Service at all levels.
    What is now needed is a political commitment sufficient to
    ensure that those skills, together with the lives of the
    women in prison, and their families, who might benefit
    from them, are not further wasted.

1 From John Howard to Michael Howard and Back Again

Prison administrators and reformers, as well as many prison campaigners have perennially found it difficult to think of women prisoners as being anything other than 'not men'. Consequently, discussions of women's imprisonment have tended to centre around questions about the extent to which the women's institutions should be different to the men's, with earlier concerns focusing on the need to protect women's (or resurrect 'fallen women's') virtue, and later ones emphasizing, on the one hand, women's rights to equality of treatment and, on the other, the state's right to exact equal penal dues from both men and women. Despite this central bifurcation, however, it is possible nowadays to trace at least four main interwoven, and difficult to separate, themes within debates about women's imprisonment.

First, and since the eighteenth century, there has been the (initially 'patriarchal' and nowadays 'feminist') concern to protect vulnerable women prisoners from sexual and gender violations.

Second, and of more recent origin, is the feminist concern to accord recognition to the specificity of women prisoners' needs without denying them parity of education, work and leisure opportunities with male prisoners.

Third, and more recently explicit, has been the state's concern to ensure that men and women prisoners suffer equality of penal pain.

Lastly, is a continuing social welfare concern about the possible damage done to the children of mothers in prison.

This chapter will now describe and discuss each of those themes separately but, intertwined and mutually transformative as they are, there will inevitably be some overlap. In the chapter's penultimate section it will be argued that all of these different strands of gendered penality have contributed to the very complex mesh of penal control which today is (in part) an end-product of a range of informal and anti-social controls inseminating women's non-penal (and pre-prison) experiences.

IN THE NAME OF THE FATHER – AND OF DECENCY

The early penal reformer, John Howard, was primarily concerned that women should be housed apart from the contaminating presence of lewd and rowdy males. Separation of female from male prisoners was also the first and over-riding concern of the nineteenth-century female prison reformer, Elizabeth Fry. That this should be so is not surprising, given the idealized images of womanhood that have been propagated from the seventeenth century onwards, and, given, also, the relatively small proportions of women in the total prison population since the end of the nineteenth century.

It has sometimes been assumed that after Elizabeth Fry had established separate and distinct regimes for imprisoned females, the women's prisons became entirely benign institutions, organized primarily for the 'gentling' of recalcitrant 'hussies' or the 'training' of 'unfortunate women', and that as a consequence, they were devoid of those harsher or more counter-productive features which have always been known to characterize the men's gaols. Yet although, in the short term, Fry's campaigning did result in better living conditions for incarcerated women, and though, too, in her earliest writings she was committed to prisoners being democratically involved in the organization of their own reform, her later blueprints for women's penal regimes prescribed several of the disciplinary techniques which became hallmarks of the mid to late twentieth-century institutions. For, as her work with women prisoners developed, Fry's concerns widened. From an initial desire to improve living conditions, and provide useful work and education, she became more concerned with developing a technology of reform which would involve constant surveillance, the erasure of individuality and strict programmes of discipline.

Dobash, Dobash and Gutteridge describe the state of the women's penal institutions in the mid-nineteenth century thus:

> By mid-century, the British had created unique and austere institutions that usually provided secure, sanitary conditions

for prisoners. Following the dictates of most reformers, they had separated women from men and appointed women warders, matrons and, later, lady superintendents to oversee the women's side. The corrupt and insanitary conditions that predominated in the late eighteenth and early nineteenth centuries had generally been replaced by new forbidding fortresses of discipline and punishment ... The new and improved prisons of this period combined degradation and humiliation with the positive elements of reform and discipline. In some ways the regimes were similar for men and women. Yet it is clear that patriarchal conceptions played a crucial role in the responses to women right from the beginning of the modern prison. The work provided for women was always predicated on assumptions about their natural skills and limitations, and the surveillance and regulation was always closer and more omnipresent than that usually directed at men. The personal and direct approach initially played an important role in some institutions. However, the impersonal and more abstract approaches increasingly gained acceptance along with an emphasis on humiliation, human accounting, hard useful labour and religious exhortation. (Dobash, Dobash, and Gutteridge 1986:61)

By 1850 two opposed trends in women's imprisonment could be detected; and they have persisted (sometimes in modified or transformed mode) right up to the present day. On the one hand it can be argued that the fundamental problem with women's prisons is that they are inappropriately modelled on institutions designed for men. On the other, it can be argued that the actual operation of the women's establishments has always been infused with both a paternalism and a *de facto* recognition that women *are* different to men. In particular, the following features of nineteenth-century women's imprisonment have survived (or resurfaced) in one form or another up to the present day: evidence of paternalistic and patriarchal attitudes on the part of the prison staff; closer surveillance and regulation of prisoners than in the men's prisons; the isolation of women from each other for much of the time, and their employment in low-paid 'women's work' or domesticity when they are in association; special accommodation for prisoners' children being incorporated into the living arrangements;

self-mutilation and suicides by prisoners; a greater number of punishments for offences against prison discipline awarded to female prisoners than to males; a narrower range of facilities than for male prisoners; and recurring concerns about sexual abuse of female prisoners by male officers.

Although by 1850 male and female prisoners were being housed in separate accommodation, the regimes for women were only very slightly different to those designed specifically for men. Admittedly, women no longer suffered the corporal punishments still inflicted on male prisoners, and in some institutions were even allowed longer periods of association; but the dominant conception of lawbreaking women as being doubly deviant – as criminals and non-conforming women – was already established in penal discourse and was to persist and have effects throughout the twentieth century.

The second half of the nineteenth century saw a gradual decrease in the number of females imprisoned, and from 1895, when 50,000 women were received into prison (Heidensohn 1985:60), until the 1970s, the prison population decreased remarkably:

> Over 33,000 women were imprisoned in 1913; by 1921 this figure had been reduced to 11,000; while in 1960 less than 2000 women were sentenced to imprisonment without the option of a fine. (Smith 1962:187)

With the decrease in the numbers of women prisoners, several of the women's wings in men's prisons were closed down. In 1902 the last of the male prisoners were transferred to Brixton and thereafter Holloway became the main prison for women. Despite the complaint of the Chairman of the Prison Commission in 1942 that not enough attention had been paid to the specific problems of women in prison, a special agenda for the discipline and treatment of women in custody was gradually and silently being established (Smith 1962:146).

Throughout the first part of the century, training in domesticity continued to be a central and most visible feature of life in the women's prisons. With the establishment of psychiatry in the prisons (Carlen 1986), however, the emergent, and, by the 1950s, dominant, discourse concerning women prisoners was that the majority of them were in need of some kind of psychiatric intervention or therapeutic treatment. It was this belief in the fundamental pathology of female prisoners that resulted in the 'new' Holloway being conceived not so much as a prison but more as a secure hospital for women in custody who, by definition, were presumed to be in need of therapy.

> In 1968 the then Home Secretary announced that it was intended to reshape the whole prison system for the custodial treatment of female offenders and that, as part of this comprehensive change, Holloway Prison was to be completely redeveloped. A central feature of this development was to be provision of comprehensive medical, psychiatric and general hospital facilities for the whole of the women's prison service ... Before the planned redevelopment could be completed, however, a number of changes had occurred in the female prison population which led to adjustments in the plan for the new Holloway. (Home Office 1985:5. See Rock 1995 for a comprehensive history of the rebuilding of Holloway Prison)

In the event, the new building was not completed until 1985.

IN THE NAME OF WOMEN AS CITIZENS

One might have assumed that once the desirability of separate institutions for women prisoners had been accepted, it would thereafter have been taken for granted that such institutions would be different to men's prisons. Yet, although in operation the women's prisons *have* always been different to the men's, the differences tend, by and large, to have been by default rather than by design; and to have stemmed from the three main and distinguishing features of women's imprisonment: the disproportionately small size of the female prison population compared with the men's; the very different composition of the female prison population, especially distinguished by fewer recidivist criminals and far more women from abroad and from ethnic minority groups at home; and the informal way in which the women's regimes have been shaped by specific and ideological conceptions of femininity and womanhood. The eighteenth and early nineteenth-century reformers who had been anxious to segregate female prisoners from males had been more concerned about protecting public decency than the women themselves. As Ann Smith put it, female prisoners had first of all been seen by reformers as potential housemaids, and then, later, as potential housewives (Smith 1962). It was not until the 1960s, when reformers started to redefine all women prisoners as potential mental patients, that an even newer generation of women's prison campaigners began to insist not only that women prisoners should be seen as having equal citizenship rights with male prisoners, but that these equal rights and responsibilities should also be tempered by a recognition of the special medical, emotional, psychological and social needs of female prisoners, which, by and large, were very different from those of male prisoners; and which emanated both from women's different biological make-up and from their different social conditioning and responsibilities.

Throughout the period of Holloway's restructuring, groups like Radical Alternatives to Prison protested against the assumption that the petty persistent offenders constituting the bulk of the female prison population at that time really needed to be contained in a secure hospital, often pointing to Professor Gibbens's 1971 observation that 'although many women in prison look as mad as mad can be, they are really reacting to prison life' (Gibbens 1971).

Gradually, the notion of the 'therapeutic prison' for women was dropped by prison administrators. But although Prison Department officials came to admit that the majority of women in prison could not be presumed to be mentally ill, staff in the women's institutions continued to invoke the stereotype of the 'mad rather than bad' female prisoner in order to justify the rigid and infantile regimes for female inmates, regimes which would not have been tolerated in the men's prisons. As the gap between the rhetoric of therapy and the reality of inadequate living conditions and debilitating regimes became more visible, newer, and more vociferous, critics began to be heard, and by the end of the 1980s a substantial body of knowledge had been built up concerning the very specific ways in which women's imprisonment in England, Wales and Scotland is different to men's, and not merely because women are biologically different to men (though that is one important difference); nor because they have a different role to play in society (though that is another). But also because the social control of women in general is *qualitatively different* to the social control of men, the main qualitative difference being that women are socially regulated in many more informal ways outside the criminal justice system than men are. In particular, they are closely controlled by familial and gender ideologies, structures and processes (see Carlen 1995). Feeley and Little (1991) have even proposed that the relatively small proportions of women in prison in most western countries have come about as the informal controls on women have strengthened and tightened. The relationships between the informal and formal social control of women will be discussed more fully in Chapter 2. They are mentioned here only because they affect first the sentencing of women and then, as a knock-on effect, the composition of the female prison population.

It has been suggested that it is because women are so closely controlled in informal ways that they actually break the law less frequently than men (Heidensohn 1986; Carlen 1988; Feeley and Little 1991). Then, because of the infrequency of women's court appearances, when they *are* accused of crimes and appear in court they are more likely to be treated as being out of place (Worrall 1981), out of mind (Allen 1987; Worrall 1990) and out of order (Carlen 1988).

In the 1980s a number of studies suggested that many poorer female teenagers and older women who appeared in the criminal courts during that decade were sentenced not primarily according to the seriousness of their crimes but more according to the courts' assessment of them as wives, mothers and daughters (Worrall 1981; Carlen 1983; Farringdon and Morris 1983; and Dominelli 1984). If they were young and their parents or state guardians believed them to be beyond control, if they were single, divorced or separated from their husbands, or if their children were in residential care, they were more likely to go to prison than women who, though their crimes might have been more serious, were living more conventional family lives. Black female offenders, because they experience racism in regard to employment and welfare policies, were (and still are) even more likely to be in the categories at risk of a custodial sentence. The latter, too, are frequently even further disadvantaged by a racist stereotyping which portrays them as being excessively promiscuous and/or aggressive.

Even when the nature of their crimes or their personal circumstances do not make convicted and poverty-stricken (or unconventional) women more prone to imprisonment than their more up-market (or conventional) sisters, there are other factors at work which push them nearer the custodial than the non-custodial end of the tariff. These include: the inability of many criminal justice personnel to 'make sense' of their poorer female clients whom they often perceive as being less rational and more devious than their male clients (see Worrall 1990); the courtroom domination by the metaphor of the 'reasonable man' which can bias the logic of the proceedings against women; and the relative scarcity of suitable non-custodial programmes and hostels for unconventional, alcoholic or poor women (as compared with the more extensive range of facilities for men in similar circumstances). Scarcity of suitable non-custodial accommodation or programmes for women on probation may result either in probation officers being reluctant to recommend mixed programmes and hostels for women who have already suffered male violence or other abuse, or in women in mixed schemes failing to complete their orders and thus being made more vulnerable to harsher sentences if they should re-offend. Other factors which make destitute women very vulnerable to the award of a custodial sentence are: the general paucity of child-care provision which makes attendance at non-custodial schemes impossible for mothers with young children; and the tendency of some report writers to recommend custody for pregnant women who are homeless or on drugs on the grounds that their material circumstances are so poor that their babies will be better off in prison (Carlen 1990).

Now this differential sentencing logic which is employed when women are in the dock has also had knock-on effects in the composition of the female prison population which is not only different to the male prison population in terms of the inmates' criminal career profiles (see below), it is also even less representative of the class structure of the total population than is the male prison population, with higher proportions coming from the non-manual classes and from Classes IV and V (Home Office 1992a:11). The National Prison Survey (Home Office 1992a) found also that, just prior to their imprisonment, women were much less likely to have been in paid employment than male prisoners, and that 12 per cent of female prisoners had never been in paid employment as compared with 6 per cent of male prisoners (Home Office 1992a:21). This is because of sentencing policies that result in women's imprisonment being what Laffargue and Godefroy (1989) have called the 'hard core of repression' – meaning that women in prison have, for most of the time since the 1960s, been gaoled either for very serious crimes, or because (despite the minor nature of their offences) their social circumstances or behaviour have been such that they have been deemed to have offended against dominant mores about appropriate female behaviour. Conversely, women seen to be living more conventional lives have often received a non-custodial penalty even for quite serious crimes (Allen 1987; Worrall 1981). Such a sentencing logic has also been thought to disadvantage young women who have been in care, women from ethnic minority groups and homeless women.

As a result of these sentencing policies (and there is some evidence that they may have changed slightly in the tougher penal climate and hard drug cultures of the late 1980s – see, for instance, Swift 1996:3) the women's prison population has been relatively small and its demographic composition skewed. It has contained even more disproportionate numbers of women who have been in care, who are from ethnic minority groups, and who are mentally ill than the men's prisons. For instance,

> A survey of 262 sentenced women prisoners and 1,751 sentenced male prisoners, published in 1994, found that a higher proportion of women prisoners had personality disorders (18% compared with 10% of men), neurotic disorders (18% compared with 10%), mental handicap (6% compared with 2%) ... 45% of women prisoners had had contact with psychiatric services before the current prison sentence compared with 6% of men. (Penal Affairs Consortium 1996:2 summarizing Maden *et al*. 1994)

The same report by the Penal Affairs Consortium also quoted from research on interviews with 200 women in three prisons which had been conducted by Morris *et al*. (1995):

> The women in this sample were broadly typical ... of female prisoners elsewhere. They were generally young, criminally unsophisticated, and were mainly in prison for property offences. Over 40% were mothers of dependent children and nearly half these mothers were single parents. Nearly 60% of the women said that they were living solely on benefits prior

to their imprisonment ... Almost a half ... reported having used drugs prior to their imprisonment and more than half of these associated their offending with drug use. Nearly one quarter described themselves as having a drink problem; two thirds of these women also reported drug use.

Nearly one quarter of the women reported harming themselves either by slashing/cutting or by attempting suicide prior to their imprisonment ... nearly half the women reported having been physically abused, and nearly one third reported having been sexually abused. (Penal Affairs Consortium 1996:2)

Given the multiple anxieties and histories of ill-health and abuse that so many women take with them into prison it is easy to see why, traditionally, there has been a tendency for prison personnel to stereotype women prisoners as ineffectual mothers who are not very bright and whose behaviour is most likely to be, at best, childlike or, at worst, deranged. Nor is it surprising that the lack of amenity in the women's penal estate is so frequently blamed on the difficulties attendant upon providing for relatively small numbers of women prisoners. This leaves prison campaigners in something of a dilemma. It is all very well to point to the paternalism towards, and infantilization of, prisoners that are characteristics of so many prison regimes for women, but it could be argued in defence of the prison officers that, just as the prisoners themselves are reacting to the conditions of prison life, so, too, are they (the prison officers) reacting to the presenting behaviour of the prisoners. How can this circle of paternalism and infantilization be broken? And can the 'too few to count' excuse (cf Adelberg and Currie 1987) about the women's prisons' inferior amenities (when compared with the men's prisons) be countered outwith acquiescence in plans for an increase in the female prison population, more mixed prisons or prison sites providing shared facilities – plans which, if realized, will almost certainly lead to a steep increase in the numbers of women being sent to prison? (see Chapter 4).

Women in Prison was founded towards the end of 1983, and, as a first step in a long-term and unfinished attempt both to reduce the female prison population and to theorize and balance the specific needs of female prisoners *as women* with those of women prisoners as citizens, set out to define what is *special* about *women's* imprisonment.

In the arena of penal politics there were already plenty of organizations which claimed to campaign for better conditions for *all* prisoners, though only one of them, Radical Alternatives To Prison, had seriously campaigned against the rebuilding of Holloway Prison in the early 1970s (see Rock 1995 for an account of that rebuilding). WIP's *raison d'etre*, therefore, was initially based on the following claims: first, that women's imprisonment is different to men's, and that the special and distinct pains of women's imprisonment have, in the main, been ignored by writers, campaigners and prison administrators; second, that women in prison suffer from discriminatory practices by administrators that result in their receiving fewer education, work and leisure opportunities than male prisoners serving comparable sentences; third, that women prisoners suffer from discriminatory practices by prison officers – as evidenced by their being subjected to closer disciplinary surveillance and regulation than male prisoners with similar criminal records; fourth, that women in prison do not receive adequate medical care for gynaecological conditions and that their special physical and emotional needs during menstruation, pregnancy and menopause are often not catered for; fifth, that mothers in prison do not receive adequate support and counselling in relation to their children outside prison; sixth, that, because there are relatively few of them, women in custody in Britain are more likely than men to be held in institutions a long way from their homes; and seventh, that *certain* women are sent to prison on the basis of a judicial logic that sentences them as *flawed women* rather than as lawbreaking citizens.

On the basis of these assumptions about the special nature of *women's* imprisonment, WIP's early campaigns centred on: increasing the public awareness of the debilitating regimes characteristic of the women's prisons; the plight of women held in extremely close confinement or under brutally harsh disciplinary regimes – like, for instance, the inmates of Durham Prison H-Wing, kept under extremes of surveillance in the 1980s because of the one person confined there who had been (wrongly) convicted of a bombing offence; and the behaviourally disturbed women of Holloway's notorious C1 Unit; the daily pains of imprisonment, and especially those specific to women and/or exacerbated by the particular regimes or practices of the different women's prisons; and the difficulties facing women upon their release from gaol.

From the outset, WIP was very aware of the disproportionate numbers of women prisoners from ethnic minority groups, and the need for liaison with organizations catering for black and foreign women in prison. Additionally, and in order to pursue strategies directed at achieving both a reduction in the prison population and an amelioration of existing unsatisfactory conditions in *all* prisons, WIP joined with other penal reform organizations to campaign against the secrecy, non-accountability to the public, censorship, and other undemocratic practices which have characterized the British prison system from the nineteenth century onwards.

In Britain, the campaigning of Women in Prison has been central to the increase in public awareness of the pains of women in penal custody. (Whether or not there has been a concomitant diminution of those pains is a much thornier question). Since 1983, many other non-statutory Groups have been campaigning or caring for women prisoners eg NACRO's WPRC (Women Prisoners' Resource Centre), WISH (Women in Special Hospitals), and Hibiscus (for female foreign nationals in prison in Britain). Each of them has a slightly different task-emphasis, but their very existence constitutes a recognition that the category 'woman-prisoner' has no global application to women prisoners' needs, all of which require analysis in the contexts of individual women's socio- biographies, as well as in the light of prevailing penal politics.

Innumerable policy documents relating to women in the criminal justice and penal systems have also been published since the mid-1980s (eg Seear and Player 1986; Women's National Commission 1991; Penal Affairs Consortium 1996; Fletcher 1997; HM Chief Inspector of Prisons 1997b; Howard League 1997a) and the media nowadays seize on (and feed on) 'women in prison' stories whenever they can.

But what has actually been achieved for women in prison? At the formal institutional level, quite a bit. In terms of any radical and fundamental improvement in women prisoners' regimes, not a lot. The 1991 National Prison Survey (Home Office 1992a) did indeed find that the women prisoners in its sample were receiving more baths, hours of work and association than the

male prisoners, and there have certainly been other innovations, such as job centres in some prisons, and programmes to
allow imprisoned mothers to see their children both more frequently and in pleasant surroundings. Yet in at least two other
areas of concern to campaigners in the 1980s there seems to
have been little progress. Take, for instance, the outcome of the
'Holloway C1 Unit' and 'Durham H-Wing' Campaigns.

Holloway's C1 Unit is for women prisoners who manifest a
variety of mental and behavioural abnormalities, though from
time to time it has been used to house women who have been
sent there because they have been seen as constituting a 'prison
control' problem, or merely because prison overcrowding meant
that there was nowhere else to put them. In 1985 C1 prisoners
were kept permanently locked in small cells, received their food
and medication through a hatch in the cell-door, and reports of
incidents of self-mutilation were horrific (see O'Dwyer *et al*.
1987). Campaigning by WIP (and others) against conditions in
the Unit was followed by the publication of two Reports (Home
Office 1985b; Clare and Thompson 1985) recommending far-
reaching changes, and on 17 July 1985 the then Home Secretary
Leon Brittan ackowledged the desirability of re-siting C1 in
purpose-built accommodation in a different part of the prison
(O'Dwyer *et al*. 1987:190). But C1 was not re-sited; and,
although the women in C1 unit are no longer locked in their
cells all day, there has been no fundamental improvement in
the situation of mentally disturbed women in prison, with many
still engaging in self-mutilation as imprisonment worsens their
already fragile emotional states (see Liebling 1992). Early in
1997 I was told by a woman who had just been released from
Holloway that when she had been there the place was so overcrowded that C1 was again being used for 'overflow' women
who were not ill at all. Later that year, in September 1997,
when I was actually talking to staff and prisoners at Holloway, a
prison officer gestured in the direction of the screams that were
resonating through the prison grounds, saying:

> 1997! I suppose someone has to have them. But is prison the
> place? I know who's doing some of that. She should never be
> in prison. (Prison Officer 14 – female)

Durham Prison's H-Wing had already housed top-security
women prisoners for 15 years when in 1989 the Lester and

Taylor Report concluded that inmates were treated less favourably than they would have been if they had been male prisoners, and that:

> If H-Wing were to remain as it is , without radical improvement we would recommend that it should be closed as soon as possible. (Lester and Taylor 1989:11)

Changes *were* made in H-Wing – in sanitation, association and facilities. But in 1993 the Prison Inspectors reported that 'Despite being less than three quarters [16 inmates] full the wing felt cramped' (HM Inspectorate 1993:25).

By 1996, when the next full inspection was held, H-Wing had undergone major refurbishment. Then, when I visited in 1997, the women were again suffering from a range of recurring problems: from overcrowding, (there were 50 inmates and the certified normal accommodation was 48); the tightening of security in the wake of the Whitemoor and Parkhurst breakouts; and new budgetary cuts which had resulted in fewer educational classes and more time spent locked in their cells. There were also continuing complaints about the claustrophobia occasioned by confinement to just one wing of a *men's* prison, as well as about the Prison Service's sporadic use of the unit as a penal warehouse for prisoners whom they could not quite decide what to do with, and who, for a variety of reasons, were seen to pose problems of control to prison management. Use of H-Wing in this way is particularly inappropriate in view of the Inspectors' 1996 concern that

> the needs of disordered women were not being fully met. There was no occupational therapy, nor in our [the Inspectors'] view sufficient professional psychiatric and psychological assistance available. (HM Inspectorate 1996:100)

And elsewhere in the women's prison system? Female prisoners are *still* imprisoned far from their homes, they *still* are subject to more petty restrictions than men, they *still* complain about the quality of the medical treatment they receive, and they *still* have a smaller range of educational, work and leisure opportunities than male prisoners. Horror stories (like, for instance, the 1996 one about the young mother at Holloway Prison who at the insistence of prison officers was forced to remain handcuffed during the funeral ceremony for her two-day old baby) *still* regularly surface in the newspapers and are confirmed by the Prison Department.

The female prison population has not been reduced. Just the reverse. In 1981 the average daily population in the women's establishments in England and Wales was 1407 (Home Office 1982); in 1993 it was 1560 (Home Office 1995a); between 1994 and 1995 it rose by 13 per cent to reach 1460 (Home Office 1996a); and by 1996 it had reached 2300 (an increase of 66 per cent in three years). Latest forecasts predict that it will rise to 3500 by 2005 (Home Office 1997a).

Young girls in criminal trouble before the age of 15 have had a particularly bad deal in so far as there have been no Young Offender Institutions specially designated for them (as there are for boys) and therefore, they have to be held with adult women. (At the time of writing a new Young Offender Unit is being planned, and the practice of imprisoning young adolescent girls with older women should cease.) Between 1992 and 1995 the use of prison custody for girls increased by 110 per cent (Howard League 1997a).

Throughout the period the women's prison population has remained at a constant 4 per cent of the total prison population, and has contained disproportionate numbers of women from British ethnic minority groups, as well as increasing numbers of foreign nationals convicted of drugs offences. Yet, despite the increase in the actual numbers of women being sent to prison nowadays, as well as the massive media attention given to women's prison issues, it could be argued that women's imprisonment in Britain is as marginalized in serious penal debate as it ever was.

In 1990 women's prisons were excluded from the terms of reference of the Woolf Inquiry (Woolf 1991) set up to report to the British government on the underlying causes of the riots which had occurred at six men's prisons during that year – even though there had also been a serious disturbance in the women's section of Risley Remand Centre. Moreover, despite the series of official and semi-official reports emphasizing that women prisoners' regimes should be different to men's, it was not until March 1997 that the Prison Department announced the setting up of a designated Unit to assess the special needs of women offenders – though the first Governor Grade appointed to head the unit left the Prison Service within three months of taking up post!

   The plain fact of the matter is that, as the composition of the female prison population is so very different to that of the male prison population, and, moreover, as in aggregate the criminal profiles of women prisoners give less cause for alarm than those of the males, there is much less official apprehension that women's prisons may erupt in riots.

   Yet, even though women prisoners pose much less of a threat to the public than do male prisoners, in the 1990s they have been made to submit to the same harsh security measures as have their counterparts in the men's prisons.

IN THE NAME OF THE STATE

It was some time in the 1980s that there were reports of criminal justice personnel beginning to mutter that if women wanted equality with men they should expect to be treated just like men when they broke the law – the implication being that women were usually treated more leniently than men – a belief which, as we have already seen, was a half-truth at best. However, this sudden official conversion to paying lip-service to a crude notion of equality for women in the criminal justice and penal systems was certainly in part responsible for many of the penal degradations suffered by women in the 1990s when, in the complete absence of a specific penal policy being developed for women, the women's institutions were inappropriately made subject to all the stringent new security measures being introduced in the men's prisons. *Inappropriately*, because women's lawbreaking and prison careers are quantitatively and qualitatively different to men's. Quantitatively different because only a very small amount of violent crime is committed by females; qualitatively different because women's crimes are committed in very different circumstances to men's.

Women in Prison in the 1990s

In 1997 16 penal establishments in England and Wales were holding women prisoners: Holloway, a closed prison in London; Styal (closed) in Cheshire; New Hall (closed) in Yorkshire; Drake Hall (open) in Staffordshire; Risley (closed) in Lancashire; Cookham Wood (closed) in Kent; Bullwood Hall

(closed) in Essex; Askham Grange (open) in Yorkshire; Low
Newton (closed) about four miles from Durham; East Sutton
Park (open) in Kent; Winchester (closed) in Hampshire;
Eastwood Park (closed), Bristol; Brockhill in Worcestershire;
Durham; Highpoint (closed) in Suffolk and Foston Hall (closed)
in Derbyshire. At Winchester, Durham, Highpoint, Risley,
Brockhill and Low Newton the women's accommodation was on
a site shared with men. Four prisons, Holloway, New Hall, Styal
and Askham Grange had Mother and Baby Units. (For a com-
prehensive description of the exact functions of each penal
establishment for women in 1997, see HM Chief Inspector of
Prisons 1997b: Appendix 4.)

Women prisoners are only categorized if they are placed in
Category A, and for all prisoners the range of amenities is
narrow – often resulting in long-term prisoners spending inor-
dinate amounts of time in one institution, and with regimes
being organized so that all prisoners are forced to comply with
the security or disciplinary requirements thought necessary for
the most disturbed or high-risk prisoner held.

For the greater part of this century, the majority of women in
prison at any one time have been there because they have been
convicted of crimes against property. Until 1995. In the Prison
Statistics England and Wales 1995 (Home Office 1996b – the
latest full statistics available at the time of writing in 1997), it
was reported that

> The main offence groups at mid-1995 were drug offences
> (30 per cent of all offences excluding offences not recorded),
> theft and fraud (29 per cent) and violence against the person
> (21 per cent) ... the main changes over the last decade have
> been that the proportion serving sentences for violent and drug
> offences has increased while the proportion serving sentences
> for theft and fraud has decreased. (Home Office 1996b:80)

But the female prison population at the same date (30 June
1996) was still only 4 per cent of the total prison population,
and although immediate custodial sentences for violence
against the person were as high as 20 per cent in the female
establishments as compared with 22 per cent in the males', the
relative totals were 355 sentences for convictions for violence
against the person being served in the women's prisons against
9230 in the men's (Home Office 1997b). Moreover, the National

Prison Survey 1991 had reported that only 11 per cent of the women in their sample had had to attend hospital as a result of a fight prior to coming to prison compared with 27 per cent of men in the sample. And overall, the social worlds of women prisoners were much less violent than those of male prisoners:

> Women convicted prisoners were less likely than men to report knowing people prior to coming into prison, who were regularly involved in fights: 28 per cent did so compare with 52 per cent of male prisoners. (Home Office 1992a:60)

In June 1995 over twice as many women as men were serving sentences for a first offence:

> Around 36 per cent of the population of adult females reported no previous convictions ... whereas for adult males the proportion was 15 per cent. (Home Office 1996a:80)

Of all women remanded in custody in 1995 only 34 per cent subsequently re-entered prison as sentenced prisoners, as compared with 47 per cent of men (Home Office, 1996b:39); and this provokes speculation as to whether women are more vulnerable to punitive custodial remands than men. Overall, it was again concluded by the Penal Affairs Consortium (1996:2) that 'most women sentenced to imprisonment are non-violent offenders and many have committed minor offences'.

In the same year the net operating costs in the female establishments per prisoner per annum were £26,675, that is, in excess of £500 per week for each female prisoner.

24 per cent of female prisoners in June 1995 were from ethnic minority groups (as compared with 17 per cent in the male) and 16 per cent were foreign nationals (as compared with 8 per cent in the male). Furthermore, it should be noted that:

> 11 per cent of British national female prisoners were black and 1 per cent were South Asian compared with 1 per cent and 2 per cent respectively of British national females aged 15–64 in the general population. (Home Office 1996b:121)

The various pathways to the women's prisons will be traced out and discussed more fully in Chapter 2. Here we go on with the story of administrative changes in the women's prisons during the last decade of the century. And, again, we take 1989 as our starting point.

Penal Discipline for Women in the 1990s – Punish and Secure

In 1989, a year after the green paper, *Punishment, Custody and the Community* had been published (Home Office 1988) the Report of the Chief Inspector for Prisons on HM Prison and Young Offenders Institution Drake Hall clearly demonstrated the difficulties prison administrators seem to have in deciding what kind of regimes are most appropriate for women prisoners. The Report made it very evident that a masculinist organizational approach stressing formality and strict adherence to rules was to be the yardstick for assessing the performance of a *real* prison, and that bereft of that yardstick the inspectors had no consistent criteria against which to assess the relevance of the regime to the women's needs (Carlen 1990). However, they did stress that, if the special needs of female prisoners for help with their complex problems (often involving not only themselves but their children too) were to be adequately met, women's imprisonment would be much more expensive than men's; and they suggested that the courts should be appraised of this.

Since 1989 the women's prison population has increased by leaps and bounds, between December 1995 and December 1996, for instance, rising by 23 per cent (Howard League 1997b). Continuous financial restrictions have resulted in a series of cuts in prison operating budgets, while the continuing steep increases in the female prison population together with the security measures introduced after the Whitemoor and Parkhurst escapes have combined to make women's open prisons more restrictive and women's closed prisons more punitive. Thus, whereas in the early 1980s the discipline of the women's penal institutions centred around a complex of concerns relating to the domesticizing and feminizing of women prisoners (Carlen 1983), by the mid-1990s the main custodial priorities were related to the maintenance of tight security and the creation of more punitive prison environments. Moreover, prison officers, who under difficult conditions had striven to engage in individual sentence planning with prisoners, had also found that their opportunities for doing so were decreased in proportion to the time they had to spend on the ever-increasing amounts of paperwork required of them.

In the 1990s changes in the women's prisons stemmed primarily from the introduction of the opposite sex posting policy in 1988, security measures taken after the Whitemoor and Parkhurst escapes, cuts in amenities as a result of decreases in prison operating budgets, and a determination on the part of Home Secretary Michael Howard that the public should be convinced that prisons are unpleasant places. Major innovations included: the introduction of male officers into the living areas of the women's prisons; the Incentives and Earned Privileges Scheme; Sentence Planning; Mandatory Drugs Testing; Dedicated Search Teams; and a generalized tightening up of security including the cessation of home leave and the manacling of prisoners on all outside visits.

Men Working in the Women's Prisons

When I first began to visit the women's prisons in the early 1980s it was a proud boast of the staff that male officers were only exceptionally brought into the living areas of the establishments. If staff shortages meant that men had to be employed in the prison, their duties were confined to manning the Gate. At that time, the arguments against employing men in women's prisons still owed much to Elizabeth Fry's concern for the protection of inmates from sexual exploitation, though modern-day supporters of single sex prisons were also beginning to marshall more up-to-date statistical evidence that one half to four-fifths of women in prison are likely already to have suffered abuse at the hands of men (see Morris *et al.* 1995; *and* HM Chief Inspector of Prisons 1997b for the most up-to-date estimates). Another widely-propagated argument against both 'mix nicks' (gaols housing male and female prisoners) and prison staff opposite sex postings contended that while they were in prison neither female nor male prisoners would want to cope with members of the opposite sex – in many cases seen as the source of their troubles outside prison.

The coming into force of the Prison Service's Opposite Sex Postings Agreement in 1988 at least put an end to mere conjecture about the consequences of men working in female prisons, though as we shall see in Chapters Two and Three, assessments of this particular innovation are very mixed, with some women prisoners still arguing that it is inappropriate for men to have unrestricted access to their cells.

In February 1996 the percentage of male officer grades
working in the women's prisons were as follows: Askham
Grange, 29 per cent; Bullwood Hall, 28 per cent; Cookham
Wood, 18 per cent; Holloway, 21 per cent; Low Newton, 8.5 per
cent; New Hall, 36.5 per cent; Pucklechurch, 19.5 per cent;
Styal 25.5 per cent (HM Prison Service, 1996a – figures not published separately for women's establishments on the same sites
as men's). Yet, whatever the virtues (or otherwise) of cross
gender postings, it has to be noted that the main consideration
in implementing the policy was not the part it might play in
any principled, consistent or holistic policy on women's imprisonment. The concern was primarily with provision of equality of
opportunity for prison staff (see Clayton 1988 in Reynolds and
Smartt 1996).

The debate about whether women should be held in wings of
men's prisons continues, and, like other recurrent issues about
women's imprisonment, nicely illustrates the complete lack of a
coherent holistic policy – with the Learmont Inquiry Report
arguing in 1995 that 'the women's Wings in male prisons should
be closed as soon as practical' (Home Office 1995b:143), and
since that time two more wings for women being opened within,
or adjacent to, male prisons. The usual justification is that
these additional wings allow women to be imprisoned nearer to
their homes. But in 1997 the rapid growth in the numbers of
women being given custodial sentences meant that women
from Essex could be found down at Eastwood Park near Bristol,
women from Hampshire up in the North East, and women from
Wales (which has no prison for women) all over the place!

Incentives and Earned Privileges Scheme

> The Incentives and Earned Privileges Scheme (IEP) began in
> July 1995 with the aim of improving prisoners' behaviour and
> performance in custody and post-release ... Prisoners are
> moved between Basic, Standard and Enhanced regimes, on
> each of which they have access to an increased number of
> privileges. (Jones 1997:1)

Categorizing prisoners according to their in-prison behaviour
(as opposed to the seriousness of the offence for which they
were convicted) is certainly not a new custodial-control device.

Various similar schemes have been used to control prison inmates ever since 'progressive stages were introduced into Gloucester Prison in 1791 (see McConville 1995:135). In 1997 the Chief Inspector of Prisons, reporting specifically on the women's prisons, described the IEP Scheme as 'a significant development in helping staff to shape prisoners' behaviour' (HM Chief Inspector of Prisons 1997b:42), thereby confirming that IEP should operate as a prison control mechanism. And in support of this view, some ex-prisoners have told me that it was fear of losing their enhanced regime status which had inhibited them from making any criticisms of the regimes or of complaining about noise, bullying or prison food or facilities while they were serving their sentences. Conversely, in June 1996 prisoners in Holloway actually told the Prison Inspectors that

> the incentives and earned privileges scheme was not working. Differences between prisons were unfair and the incentives offered weren't appropriate. They said that the reviews weren't happening and that the move to place prisoners on the basic level was abused by some staff with grudges. (HM Chief Inspector of Prisons 1997a:30)

The prisoners' entry level to the scheme in the women's prisons I visited in 1996 and 1997 depended very much on which prison they were in, as did the range and type of privilege associated with each regime. Thus IEP, as it was operating in 1997, failed to offer equality of opportunity to women prisoners and, in so doing, also violated the previously-held notion that a prisoner goes to prison *as* punishment rather than *for* punishment. Certainly, and as will be seen in Chapter 3, mixed views on the operation of the Scheme were also held by both staff and inmates in prisons other than Holloway. (For a brief description of the national evaluation of IEP see Liebling and Muir 1997).

Sentence Planning

> The Prison Service has introduced formal sentence planning for all prisoners serving over twelve months in custody, but in many of the establishments for women, sentence planning is not fully in place and is not given sufficient priority. (HM Chief Inspector of Prisons 1997b:124)

The Chief Inspector also found that the sentence planning forms had been recognized in 1995 as being inappropriate for women, that there was no formal custody planning for women on remand, that many staff had never had training in sentence planning, and that, even when women had been involved in planning their sentences, their constant moves round the system tended to undermine the continuity and coherence which should be central to the whole logic of the scheme.

Yet, as we shall see later in these pages, in 1997 several Governors and many officers had an even different tale to tell – of a chaos and confusion in the women's system which could be explained almost entirely by the overcrowding occasioned by the rapid female prison population explosion of the 1990s, a situation which left staff little time to cope with the demands of increased paperwork, increased assessments (for 'risk' and sentence planning), the development of prisoner 'compacts' (or contracts) and demanding 'personal officer schemes'.

Mandatory Drug Testing

> Powers to require prisoners to provide a sample for drug testing purposes were introduced as part of the Criminal Justice and Public Order Act in January 1995. (Prison Service Security Group 1996:2)

Mandatory Drug Testing (MDT) was introduced in prisons in 1995 and is undertaken for the following five reasons: as part of a monthly 10 per cent random drug testing of the population of a prison; on suspicion that a prisoner has illicitly used a controlled drug; as part of a frequent testing ordered at the adjudication of a prisoner found guilty of a drug-related offence; as part of the risk assessment when a prisoner is being granted temporary release or transferred to lower security; and upon first reception, or on transfer and admission to a different prison (Prison Service Security Group 1996:2–3). According to the Prison Service Security Group

> The MDT Manual allows women's prisons a high level of discretion to create their own procedures to meet the perceived threat of adulteration in each establishment. As a consequence, sample taking practices do vary between establishments. At Holloway women are allowed complete privacy in a

closed cubicle. Other prisons have adopted a system whereby the cubicle has a stable door arrangement; the bottom half is closed and the top half left open. The woman is asked to place one hand on the door whilst holding the sample cup with the other. In all cases the woman is allowed to wear a gown so that observation of the genitalia whilst urinating is not possible. Male staff are not allowed to collect samples from women. (Prison Security Group 1996:3–4)

Six comments.

First of all it should be noted that the 'closed cubicle' system in Holloway was introduced only after both staff and prisoners had objected to a system involving officers watching women while they were urinating.

Secondly, although the mode of testing described above may seem unexceptional to many people, the Chief Inspector of Prisons was told that women who had previously been sexually abused did take exception to it:

> Many of the women we spoke to complained, not of being tested but of having to provide a sample of urine while being observed by a prison officer. In some cases this was felt to be comparable to and bring back memories of previous sexual assault. (HM Chief Inspector of Prisons 1997b:136)

Third, there are claims that with the introduction of MDT some prisoners switched from cannabis to opiates because they pass through the body more quickly and therefore are less likely to be detected by a urine test.

Fourthly, it is doubtful to what extent it is appropriate for prisons to put so many resources into 'eradicating drugs in prison' (HM Prison Service 1996b:11) by this especially costly but high-profile method ('it's a gimmick' – Governor Grade, 1996) when drug-usage is so widespread outside and, according to the Chief Inspector 'there is an absence of an *overall detoxification strategy implemented systematically and consistently across the female estate* (HM Chief Inspector of Prisons 1997b:137).

Fifth, some prison staff argue that there are far fewer drug-related incidents in the women's prisons than in the men's, and 'that women's dealing is less organized and often based on sharing among acquaintances rather than on profit and intimidation (HM Chief Inspector of Prisons 1997b:134).

l with reference to the points raised by the five fore-
ervations about MDT, two governor grade staff and
nain grade officers told me in 1996–97 that they
thoug MDT was a complete waste of resources because it was
impossible to stop drug usage in prisons, and that while they
would never condone the presence of illicit drugs in their establishments, they did think that the present high priority given to
drug detection was a misdirected use of resouces, especially in
the women's establishments.

Dedicated Search Teams

Both Woodcock (Home Office 1994) and Learmont (Home
Office 1995b) recommended that dedicated search teams
should be established in prisons and that they should be
assisted in their prison searches by dogs trained in the detection of firearms, explosives and drugs. As we have already seen,
the mode of dress of the Dedicated Search Team at Holloway
attracted unfavourable comment in 1996, and in 1997 the Chief
Inspector of Prisons found that, in the women's prisons,

Many managers and staff felt that personal searching was one
of the most difficult areas to manage. One specific difficulty
was the concealment, particularly of drugs but also other
illicit articles, in prisoners' vaginas. Internal searching by
prison staff is not permitted even when there is a very strong
suspicion that prisoners have concealed contraband inter-
nally. Prison staff can require prisoners to bend or squat ...
but none of the staff to whom we spoke considered that
this was at all effective with women prisoners. (HM Chief
Inspector 1997b:46)

None the less, as late as 1997 some women prisoners *were* being
made to bend over during strip searches, and as we shall see
throughout this book, strip searching, although accepted as an
inevitable and justifiable part of prison life by many prisoners,
is seen as a violation of personal autonomy and modesty by
others, especially those who have never taken drugs, who have
suffered sexual abuse, are from countries where feminine
modesty is rigorously enforced, or who already agonize over
their body shape. To these latter groups of women strip searching can cause deep distress, and, in some cases, provoke
extreme acts of resistance to what is experienced as an assault.

In his *Thematic Report* the Chief Inspector argued that '[T]he reasons justifying the use of dedicated search teams in male establishments apply equally to secure establishments for females' (HM Chief Inspector of Prisons 1997b:47). Many informed commentators, including some prison staff, would beg to differ.

One of the greatest causes of resentment in the women's prisons of the late 1990s, and one that will run through this book as a most insistent refrain, is that dedicated search teams, like many of the other new and restrictive measures of the 1990s, were set up after extreme breaches of security (escapes) in the *men's* prisons, and that there have never been any comparable threats to security in the women's prisons. Thus, the increased emphasis on strip searching in women's prisons is but another example of the way in which the women's prison system is carelessly treated as being nothing more nor less than a codicil to the men's. And, again, this deplorable state of affairs persists because, despite all the adverse publicity the women's prisons have attracted in recent years, there still is no woman-wise, principled, coherent and holistic strategy for management of women's imprisonment.

Handcuffing

> Handcuffs had a history of use that paid no heed to age or sex ... There was, also a special mode of restraint reserved to women called 'hobbling', which consisted 'in binding the wrists and ankles of a prisoner and then strapping them together behind her back' (Priestley 1985, quoting Maybrick 1905)

The increased security measures which followed upon the escapes from Whitemoor and Parkhurst men's prisons affected the women's prisons in many ways. Fewer prisoners were allowed to work outside, strip searching became more frequent, mandatory drug testing was implemented, and handcuffing on visits to outside hospitals, family and other appointments became the norm rather than the exception for prisoners in some establishments. Indeed, stopping the cuffing of women in labour and at other hospital appointments became the *cause celebre* of anti-prison campaigners in 1996 and 1997, a cause which the Chief Inspector unequivocally backed in his *Thematic Report*:

Prior to the Woodcock inquiry women prisoners were hand-cuffed only in exceptional cases. Since then the increased focus on security and the application of policies arising from incidents at high security prisons for men to all prisoners, including women, has placed unwarranted restrictions on woman under escort. The vast majority of women are not an escape risk, nor do they pose serious danger to the public.

We have heard of women refusing hospital treatment for serious conditions because they did not want to be cuffed in public. For similar reasons women have not attended child custody hearings. In the latter circumstances, they felt, not unreasonably, that appearing in handcuffs might influence decisions about the custody of their children. Regrettably, there is still no clear statement from the Prison Service about the policy of handcuffing women. (HM Chief Inspector of Prison 1997b:45)

But the Prison Service has now at least issued Instruction 5/97 which 'instructs that women admitted to NHS hospitals to give birth should not be handcuffed from the time of their arrival until they leave' (*ibid*).

Prison Transport

A recurring complaint from the women whom I interviewed was about how unsafe, ill or faint they had felt when being transported in the prison vans comprised of what are known as 'sweatboxes'.

I had a court appearance every two months and I was transported in a sweatbox, like a travelling cell. It's very claustrophobic, you can't see out of the windows, and the ventilation in them is very poor. No seat belts and the seats are shiny. Now I had to travel all the way from Yorkshire to Highbury [London] in one of those. It's noisy, it rattles. I mean, it's literally a box with a hard seat – for a four and a half, five hour journey! Transport from one prison to another is also terrible because you are handcuffed all the way. (Liz, aged 19)

When I came from court to here [prison] I had to come in one of those vans and I passed out. I was in the little cubicle sort of thing, no seat belt, and I passed out and slipped down.

I scraped all my shoes and I've got a scar on that foot. They said that I just passed out. I was beginning to feel hot, then I couldn't breathe, and then I just passed out. They called an ambulance but I didn't know because I was still out for the count. They said it took a long time for me to come round. By the time I came round the ambulance was already there and my blood pressure had gone sky high. (I hadn't got my blood pressure pills with me because I had not been expecting to go to prison; I had been expecting to go home that night, you know.) I was taken to the hospital, but once I come out of the hospital it was back into that van again! The two security people were worried sick – that the same thing was going to happen again. They said, 'If you feel just a little bit faint, let us know and we'll pull up'. And they said that they would put in a report that I should not travel in one of those vans again. (Rosalie, aged 57)

IN THE NAME OF THE CHILDREN

It is a central argument of this study that when women go to prison, a fine (and scarcely definable) mesh of the informal controls that silently coerce and define women outside prison is immediately intertwined with formal penal sanctions; with the result women usually experience a much heavier penal burden than men. The most obvious effect these informal controls have on women's imprisonment is manifested in the pain that imprisoned mothers experience as a result of being deprived of their children while in gaol (Carlen 1983; Shaw 1992) and this very specific maternal pain will be discussed again in Chapter 3. Here, let us just look at the statistical picture.

It is very difficult to get accurate figures of the number of women prisoners who have children under 16 who were actually living with them at the time of their admission to prison. Some mothers fear that, if they admit to having children, both the children and their carers will become recipients of unwelcome attentions by Social Services, and that the children may even be taken into local authority care.

In 1985 NACRO reported that over 1600 children under the ages of 16 had mothers in prison (NACRO 1985), and there have been various surveys since, either based on one prison (eg

Prison Reform Trust 1996 on Holloway) or on a random sample
drawn from all the women's prisons (eg Home Office 1992a).
The most up-to-date and comprehensive figures available are to
be found in the data provided by the Prison Department for the
Chief Inspector's *Thematic Report*. This data was collected from
all women in the 15 prison establishments holding females in
October and December 1996 and it revealed that:

> 55% of all women had at least one child under sixteen years
> of age (83% of those with children). Over a third of the
> mothers had one child or more under 5 years old. 43%
> had children between 11 and 15 years and 42% had chidren
> 16 years or over. 4% of the women had a child of up to
> 18 months old in the prison with them. (HM Chief Inspector
> of Prisons 1997b: Appendix 3)

But it is not clear how many of the mothers of children under
16 had their children living with them immediately prior to
their imprisonment. The National Prison Survey 1991 (Home
Office 1992a:17) which was based on a random sample of 20 per
cent of the female prison population (and 10 per cent of the
male) interviewed in January and February 1991 found that:

> One third of all prisoners had dependent children living with
> them just before they came into prison, with the proportion
> much higher among female prisoners (47%)than among male
> prisoners (32%). (*ibid*)

Some of the most interesting findings of this Survey were in
relation to the differences between the domestic responsiblities
of male and female prisoners both prior to their imprisonment
and while they were serving sentence. For instance:

> Male prisoners were more likely than female prisoners to
> have been living with their parents prior to imprisonment
> (20 per cent as against 11 per cent). This was not simply
> because the male prison population is somewhat younger
> than the female population; in all age groups up to the age of
> thirty male prisoners were more likely than female prisoners
> to have been living with parents. By contrast, female prison-
> ers were much more likely than male prisoners to have been
> living with dependent children and no other adult (14 per
> cent against 1 per cent. (Home Office 1992a:18)

Furthermore:

> There were considerable differences, between men and women with dependent children in the child care arrangements that had been made. Male prisoners with dependent children usually said that their spouse or partner (64%) was involved ... By contrast, of female prisoners with dependent children, just 19 per cent said that at least one of their children was being looked after by their spouse or partner, and 4 per cent by an ex-spouse or ex-partner. (Home Office 1992a:17)

In fact, and as will be illustrated in Chapter 2, it is a distinct feature of women's imprisonment that many women in prison are expected, or feel obliged, to try to run their homes and families while they are in prison. By contrast, there is some evidence that male prisoners are much more likely to expect to be shielded from family and domestic burdens while they are serving their sentences (cf Fishman 1990).

In 1997 there were four mother and baby units (MBUs) in prison establishments – at Askham Grange, Holloway, New Hall and Styal. Between them they provided 68 places for mothers with babies (up to the age of nine months in the 17 places at Holloway Prison, and up to 18 months at the other MBUs). Much of the more recent and detailed investigative work on conditions in mother and baby units has been done by the Howard League (see for instance, Howard League 1993, 1994, 1996). The most worrying of their findings are as follows:

- that in one MBU in September 1995 11 out of 17 mothers (ie 65%) had been imprisoned for non-violent offences (Howard League 1996:7)
- that 'one prison stated that the prison budget only allowed babies half the amount allocated for adults. This amounted to 70p per day' (Howard League, 1996:9) (Four years previously, in a very critical Report of a 1990 Inspection of MBUs, a Department of Health Inspection Team had tellingly remarked that they had 'understood that both the budget and the variety of meals provided for mothers was less than at the male prisons' (Department of Health, 1992:13)
- Since the tightening of security after the Woodcock Report (Home Office 1994) babies have been searched more

frequently, the searching involving both rub-down and strip searches. (Howard League 1996:10)

Other commentators on babies in prison have drawn attention to the paucity of stimulating materials for children (Catan 1988, 1992), the difficulties that mothers face in establishing their own routines for babies while they themselves are subject first and foremost to the prison's routines, and also to the traumas of separation when the child is no longer allowed to stay in the prison (either because it has reached the 'leaving' age, or is taken from the mother as a punishment for the mother's transgression of a prison rule).

Finally, it has to be noted that while prison rules and the thin geographical spread of the women's prisons make it more difficult than it need be for *all* women in custody to maintain outside relationships, they make it particularly difficult for mothers to maintain good quality contact with their children. Furthermore, many of the problems outlined above are likely to be amplified when the mother is a foreign national (Heaven 1996).

THE TURNING OF THE GENDER SCREW

Imprisonment not only punishes mothers by inducing guilt and anxiety about children left 'abandoned' outside prison while they are serving their sentences. It also multilaterally punishes all women prisoners by reversion to an almost mediaeval targeting of their bodies as sites subversive of the state's power to punish. As the twentieth century draws to a close, every part of a woman prisoner's existence is laid out for physical, medical, psychiatric, legal and social-work analysis. Concomitantly, the disciplinary and security paraphernalia in women's prisons creatively harness a wide spectrum of women's bodily and emotional fears to a penal process that is ever-innovative, ever-revisionist and ever-transformative in its modes of inspection and repression. It is innovative because it constantly has to adapt to the effects that changing political and social conditions have on the penal system. It is revisionist because, as prisons are essentially places directed at the maintenance of a state of permanent closure, (they have no other organizational product), all innovative influences have to be 'closed off' as soon as they really threaten to weaken the fundamental power of that closure (see Sparks 1995 for an account of the threateningly innovative Barlinnie Special Unit and the possible reasons for its abolition in 1994). The task of the next two chapters will be to show how the contradictory political impulses provoked by those conditions have been responsible for fashioning a sledge-hammer of a penal system that is excessively harsh in the amount of penal pain it inflicts, wasteful of human endeavour, and very gender-specific. Even so, and as I will argue in Chapter 4, women's imprisonment in England could be different ... and there are several socially sound and penologically judicious strategies which might lead to its eventual abolition.

– AND BACK AGAIN

1905   Testimony of Mrs F. E. Maybrick in Priestley (1985:203)

I was never allowed to forget that, being a prisoner, even my body was not my own. It was horrible to be touched by unfriendly hands, yet I was compelled to submit – to be undressed and searched.

1997   Testimony of Lindis Percy (private communication with the author)

I have reluctantly tolerated strip searching whenever I have had to. However, last time in Low Newton I gently declined. It is utterly degrading, humiliating and frankly disgusting. I'm sure it is an issue in prisons. I cannot imagine what it feels like for women who have been abused etc.

So we arrive in prison, often shell-shocked, angry etc. etc. and are immediately told to take our clothes off. Some officers of course are skilled and caring and help the process by being sensitive also. Nevertheless, it is foul.

At Low Newton I was immediately put 'on report', put in a cell with another woman (not even a rub-down search), next day charged and heard. Sorted.

Holloway is Holloway. I was put 'on report'. Seen by a doctor who said, 'Look, just do it. They can/will do horrible things to you'. I caught the word 'horrible' and asked what she meant, but it got lost as I was moved back to the pen I had been put in when on report. The doctor thought I should go to the medical wing because of a bad ear infection, and also, as I had lost nearly a stone in police custody, to monitor my weight. I hadn't eaten all that time because of being switched off by large doses of antibiotics and increasingly stronger pain relief. I'm not used to any tablets.

I was taken up to the Wing by two very unpleasant officers. When we got there people seemed to be rather scurrying about and I noticed the women's hatches on the doors being closed momentarily. I wondered why. Then I was put in a cell with a bed fixture and a locker and a concrete floor. I was followed in by four officers and a nurse. I was suddenly alarmed by this and realized they were going to force strip search. 'You can do this the easy way or the hard way' etc. I again said that I declined, that I was on Report and how they must charge and I would then be heard. I was being cornered. I asked for the legal authority, could I speak to a doctor?. 'No she's busy'. Appealed to the nurse to intervene. She stood silently, her role was to look at 'lumps, bumps and tatoos'. I asked on whose authority this was being ordered; 'higher authority'. And then one of the officers (woman, I hasten to add – at least they did that bit correctly) said 'RIGHT!' and I was forced on to the concrete floor – terribly cold – and they systematically removed all my clothes. I didn't kick, scream or bite – just sobbed and sobbed in total shock and disbelief as to what was happening. I was left on the concrete floor half naked as they all withdrew. It felt, and I maintain was, an indecent assault ...

As a result of the indecent assault I was totally off my food and didn't drink a lot either – utterly traumatized. I have tried to think of a compromize as this has got locked and it's very clear to me that it's about 'You will comply with prison rules. We are in charge here and you will ...' etc. etc. Nothing to do with a genuine concern that I might have something on me. I wasn't even searched in police custody, nor were my possessions. It would be totally against everything I believe in and hold dear to carry anything. I attend Quaker meetings and have done so for about 17 years.

So I went into a state of fear I suppose at the thought of this all happening again. Food/drink aren't important. What is important is the thought of more violence and of being indecently assaulted again... . My family organized an independent doctor to come in. He has written an extremely powerful letter to the Governor saying that what they are doing amounts to gratuitous sadism – which is what it is. Awful!

The [prison] doctor had assured me that I would not be strip-searched [again] and when he saw me he said that the hearing would be on the Unit.

The officers came in and in fact the hearing was not to be heard on the Unit. The Assistant Governor wanted it on the Block. I still didn't think they would force me. Well, they did. Absolutely shocking – five officers this time and two waiting as I arrived – with surgical gloves on ...

What a system! There have been four cell fires since I have been here. Women cutting up and very disturbed behaviour. Officers – some very skilled and very good, and many who need extra in-service training. Or something! (Lindis Percy:27 February 1997)

A Prison Officer's Comments – when showing me round a women's prison in the South of England in February 1997

We have people in here aged 15 to 83. Yes, we have three fifteen year-olds here at present, and we have an old lady of 83 in for receiving. We have another old lady of 77 who lives in an old people's home, and every so often she goes out and gets drunk and gets sent here – usually for assaulting a policeman. Can you imagine him standing up in court and saying that this little old lady who is under 5 foot tall has assaulted him?

We have women in here we do nothing for. One is going out soon and I shall have her on my conscience. She is in for attacking her husband and also for setting fire to her children and husband, and we've done absolutely nothing for her. In fact, we've done sod all for her.

This is a strip cell which is also a punishment cell. See the food and burn marks on the ceiling? They realized they could smuggle in lighters up their vaginas and back passages, and at least make enough smoke to set off the alarms. See? Just a mattress and a night shirt, and that's the best we can do in the 1990s! It must have been like that two hundred years ago. (Prison Officer 24 – Male)

2 Women, Gender and Imprisonment

On 2 January 1990 at Wakefield Crown Court a first-time offender, (let's call her Sharon Smith), was given six months youth custody after pleading guilty to helping other people steal £4000 worth of goods from the store where she was checkout assistant. She became pregnant soon after the offence came to light and, by the time she was sentenced, had a ten week-old daughter. She was allowed to take the baby into prison with her. The media furore which greeted her imprisonment, however, was neither because this was her first offence, nor because she was a youthful offender – two factors which could have been expected to result in the non-custodial sentence recommended by Probation. What caused the case to become national news for the two weeks prior to appeal were the remarks made by the judge who, in sentencing her, told Ms Smith that he had to impose a custodial sentence to deter other young women from becoming pregnant in order to avoid imprisonment. (Though he admitted that he had no grounds for assuming that Ms Smith herself had become pregnant with such intent.)

On appeal the sentence was reduced to probation and further comment was made on the trial judge's handling of the case.

> Unfortunately the judge also saw fit to unburden himself on the subject of young women who might become minded to avoid pregnancy to escape sentence. The impression was left that the judge was using the case to illustrate the unwisdom of young women embarking on pregnancy, which was, to say the least, unfortunate. (Lord Lane, Lord Chief Justice, reported in *The Guardian* 16 January 1990)

Because British justice is supposed to be not only gender-neutral but also colour-blind (Criminal Justice Act 1991 s95; Home Office 1992b) the Lord Chief Justice (quite properly) did not refer to the fact that Sharon Smith was black. Since 1990 the population of the women's prisons has rocketed, with lone mothers and black women disproportionately represented within it.

I chose to open this discussion of 'Women, Gender and Imprisonment' with the example of a black British, teenage, single mother employed in the retail trade because her court-room story encapsulates all of the main politico-economic gender conditions which in part fashion the forms, functions and meanings of women's imprisonment at the end of the twentieth century. Those major politico-economic gender conditions inhere in the fundamental class and racist inequities which systematically manifest themselves in: the operation of national and international labour, and illicit commodities, markets; the institutions of marriage, family and welfare; and the discourses of approved femininities within which conventionally gendered bodies and selves are fashioned – and unconventionally gendered bodies and selves are assessed and judged. Traces of them all will surface again and again as, in this chapter, we examine: the massive increases in the number of women sent to gaol; the most usual pathways to the women's prisons; how all women are informally, but very closely, regulated by economic, familial and other taken-for-granted social and anti-social controls in their lives outside prison; and the debilitating ways in which these extra-mural and anti-social regulatory modes inseminate women's experiences of penal confinement. Then, in Chapter 3 we will see how these same informal controls were contextually transformed and tightened in the 1990s, to give specifically-gendered meanings to what politicians and administrators insist are gender-neutral control strategies devised only to maintain prison security.

Yet, although it is an argument of this book that the effects of the most recent security measures are *not* gender-neutral, there is certainly no desire to imply that the tightening of security in all prisons was done with any misogynous intent.

Rather, the overall aim of this chapter and the next is to demonstrate that a sytematically-gendered socio-penal *configuration* – of informal social controls which women experience (though differently according to class and ethnicity) outside prison, with the formal penal regulations enforced within prisons – creates gender-specific and disproportionate pain to women in custody. This point will be returned to, and expanded, in Chapter 4 where one of the main arguments to be developed will be that such penal pain, in being discriminatory and destructive, is also anti-social.

WHY HAS THE 1990S SEEN A STEEP INCREASE IN WOMEN'S IMPRISONMENT?

A Prison Governor's Reply

There are a tremendous amount of principled people in the Prison Service, at all ranks, at all levels, but they feel very under-valued, very under-resourced, and very frustrated because they feel that what they had that was good is never going to come back again while there is this approach to sending people to prison for longer, for less serious offences, to get them off the streets. There is no question about it, you only have to look at the rising prison population.

The amount of reported crime is not significantly higher than it used to be but the number of prison sentences handed out is higher. Obviously there has been a shift to a greater use of imprisonment, and particularly, dramatically, for women. It could be this is a sort of anti-feminist approach by the courts that says, 'Well, if you women want equality, you've got to take it'.

It could be that the pressure on a lot of women is much greater now than it was before; to survive without a male partner, and the pressure upon them is financially greater. Women have achieved independence and in order to maintain it in some cases, they've had to commit crime.

Another reason could be that we've got a larger number of female police officers in the system at the moment. So maybe they are not so sympathetic as a male officer.

We've always had violent women around, but men in the past didn't necessarily go and report an offence against them by a woman because that wouldn't be macho, whereas these days it's probably more acceptable for them to do so.

It could also be that women have in the past more often gone down the mental hospital path. Well, that's been shut-off to many people because of the cuts in secure accommodation. So now, perhaps more women go through the criminal justice system who should be in the mental hospitals.

I cannot understand the thinking behind dishing out eight, ten, twelve-year sentences to foreign women coming into this country as mules [drug couriers]. Why? What does it achieve? It's a drain on the tax payer, and it doesn't demonstrate that we're hard on drugs, because the women coming across here never believe they're going to get caught.

Often they come under duress. They're from Third World countries where they've got children to support. They may well be widowed, or been abandoned with children. The amount of money they get paid is, by our standards, peanuts, but could support their family in Nigeria for two or three years. And they come across here, as I say, under duress or the lure of quick money. I have a large percentage of Nigerian women in [the prison I work in], who say that on the flight [they were on] there were more than one of them, but that they were fingered in order to let the other ones go through. So, in a sense these women may be the victims, as well as the perpetrators, of crime. (Governor No 2 – Female)

A Board of Visitors Member's Reply

My own view is that if they'd had a decent lawyer they wouldn't be in prison. I think their cases have been desperately rushed, and haven't been dealt with properly. Sometimes you think, 'I haven't been given the whole story here', but when you read their files you find that it actually bears out the tale. And we are surprised at the severity of some of the sentences being imposed on youngsters now.

Two weeks ago, I met a delightful girl here who was working in the kitchen, and serving 18 months. She was a student, never been in trouble, delightful family and she'd been in a fight in a pub. She was sentenced to 18 months and her boyfriend got two years. I mean, it was just a pub brawl, no weapons had been involved, and the [male] probation officer here was very surprised too. (BOV 3 – female)

Prison Officers' Replies

Carlen: Magistrates and judges insist to me that nowadays they don't send women to prison for trivial crimes...

Pris.Off: Well they do. We still have people coming in for not paying their poll tax. I can't believe women are going to gaol for not paying poll tax. For such short sentences. Women come for five days. But even if they come in for a month, it doesn't make sense. A society that claims to be so sophisticated! And then they send people to gaol for five days, ten days, a fortnight or a month. I cannot believe that's happening for a tax which everybody, I think any right-minded person, thought was an unfair tax in the first place. Then, non-payment of fines. Non-payment of a television licence! I know they don't come to gaol for non-payment of a television licence, but they do go to court and get fined, and nine times out of ten, it's obvious, if you can't afford to pay the television licence, you haven't got a hope in hell of paying the fine. So they come to gaol for not paying the fine. Now, that doesn't make sense to me. (Prison Officer 13 – male)

Pris.Off: We admitted a girl of 19 yesterday. She was four or five months pregnant and she was asthmatic. She had stolen £5 and it was her first offence. OK, it was from the old people's home where she worked... not very nice. But even so! They might as well just go out and pick anyone off the street and send them to prison. What are the judges thinking of? Where is it going to stop? It makes a farce out of the whole thing. (Prison Officer 20 – female)

Prisoners' Comments

I've seen girls in Brockhill for poll tax, which I find unbelievable. They brought one girl in for [owing] £300 poll tax. She got thirty six days. They took her four children, who were all under eight, into care for that time. There were also girls in there for television licence fines. I just can't believe it. (Kay, aged 46)

Now the courts put women away quicker – for silly little shoplifting offences and things like that. Years ago you would have got a slap on the wrist, but now they are putting more women away and Holloway is just overcrowded. There are some people in there, you think, 'What on earth are they doing here?' But they've got nothing outside and the courts have nowhere else to put them, so they're thinking, 'Right, put them in prison – epecially the younger girls'. (Carol, aged 37)

As we saw earlier, the female prison population has risen by leaps and bounds in the 1990s, the most staggering rise being that of 57 per cent between December 1992 and December 1995 (Penal Affairs Consortium 1996:2) (Over the same period the male population increased by 29 per cent). How can the increase in the women's prison population be explained? Four main answers tend to be given: (1) more women are committing violent crimes; (2) more women who would not previously have gone to prison are going in the 1990s because of their increasing involvement with drugs; (3) more *black* women are going to prison, and therefore racism is the key to the increase; (4) prison is being used to incarcerate the same social categories of women that it always has – the destitute, the most obviously gender-deviant, and the mentally-disturbed – but the numbers of women presenting themselves in these categories have increased with the growing economic inequalities of the 1980s and 1990s. (For growing inequalities in general, see Barclay 1995; on women and poverty, see Glendinning and Millar 1992; and on financial difficulties on release from prison see Hagell, Newburn and Rowlingson 1995).

Are Women Committing More Serious Crimes? More Specifically, Are They Committing More Violent Crimes?
The popular press have been in no doubt as to how that question should be answered. According to the tabloids and some magazines, women, especially younger women, are becoming more violent, acting increasingly like their more crime-prone brothers and thus, so the fable goes, are once more reminding us that the 'the female is deadlier than the male'. Criminologists known to be working on the subject (as well as women in the campaigning groups) are daily inundated with calls from journalists wanting more information about 'wimmin and violence'. My own experience is most probably not atypical. When, a couple of years ago, I decided to log 'women and crime' calls, I received seven phone calls in three days from enquirers who wanted me to provide them (variously) with: 'up-to-date figures on all-girl gangs'; 'explanations for female muggers'; 'a profile of the kind of women who steal babies'; an estimate of 'how much a prostitute can earn in one night?' a guess at 'what makes Rose [a recently-sentenced female serial killer] tick?' and, in one case, 'some interview contacts with violent [*sic*]

women'. (I was unable to oblige in all cases – even, self-denyingly, the last!)

Yet, despite the certainties and more prurient insinuations of the hacks, (analyses of the official criminal statistics suggest that the rise in the female prison population cannot be totally explained by recorded increases in women's violent (or other serious) crime.

In 1996 the proportion of female prisoners under sentence for crimes of violence against the person was indeed (at 20 per cent) only 2 per cent less than the proportion of male prisoners under sentence in the same offence category. Moreover, and as Harry Fletcher (1997:5) points out:

> It is undoubtedly the case that the level of convictions of violence against the person has increased among women. The number rose from 5,000 to 9,000 during the 10 year period to 1994 and then fell back to just below 8,000 in 1995.

But what also needs to be noted is that the 1996 British Crime Survey (Home Office 1996C) clearly indicates that women's violence has different characteristics to men's, and is much less likely to be randomly directed towards strangers (Fletcher 1997:6). And, although I am not prepared to join Fletcher and others in implying that domestic and acquaintance violence is less serious than other types of violence, it has to be admitted that reports of violence between acquaintances does not fill the public with the same terror that stranger violence does; and is generally considered to be more understandable and less threatening – even though it may still be seen as being inexcusable. On the other hand, there are certainly arguments and evidence that peer-related assaults between young males are likely to be viewed by both police and courts as being less serious than those between young women (Carlen 1983; Hudson 1984; Loader 1996). If we consider all female crime, moreover, Fletcher's most telling points are that between 1993 and 1995 there were decreases in both serious and less serious crimes committed by women; and that, therefore, '*The female prison population has...risen steeply whilst serious convictions have actually fallen*' (Fletcher 1997:4, his emphasis). He adds:

> An explanation offered in Prison Statistics 1995 is that the proportion of women serving longer sentences has increased,

so that 41 per cent were serving 3 years or more in 1995, compared to 19 per cent 10 years earlier. Sentence lengths are
generally one month longer than the previous year. The proportion serving time for violence and drugs increased whilst
the proportion for theft and fraud fell. *Nevertheless, over the
whole of 1995, over 70 per cent of the total numbers of women received
into custody had committed offences of theft, handling or other less
serious matters. The remainder were in prison for violence, burglary,
robbery or drug related offences.* (Fletcher 1997:4. Emphasis added)

*Is There an Increased Punitiveness Towards Lawbreaking Women
Because There Has Been a Regulation Panic About Drugs Importation
and The Number of Violent Crimes That are Drink And Drug-Related?*
Given that there has been what Brain and Parker (1997) have
called a 'regulation panic' about the increase in drink and drug-
taking and drink and drug-related crimes in recent years, it is
very likely that the general climate of panic about drug usage has
affected the sentencing of women, and that the longer sentences
imposed have increased the numbers of females in prison at any
one time. Penny Green's research lends some support to this view:

> The evidence from this research (and from Home Office and
> Prison Department Statistics..) suggests that approximately
> 80 per cent of all imprisoned couriers are men. Earlier esti-
> mates had placed the percentage of women considerably
> higher – virtually all journalistic and pressure group interest
> in couriers has been on women – assisting a distorted percep-
> tion. What is significant, however, is that female drug cour-
> iers account for approximately 20 per cent of the UK female
> prison population, whilst male couriers account for only
> 4 per cent of the total male population. (Green 1996: 15)

Moreover, writing in 1997, Fletcher agrees that

> From 1985 to the current period there was an increase in the
> number of women convicted of offences of violence…and at
> least 70 per cent was either drug or alcohol related. (Fletcher
> 1997:1)

Nonetheless, and as Fletcher himself emphasizes, it is still the
case that the majority of women received into custody under
sentence serve short terms for theft, handling and fraud. Given
the most recent demographic profiles of women in custody

(Morris 1995; HM Chief Inspector of Prisons 1997b), and the fact that their criminal histories tend to be much shorter and less criminally serious than men's, it is arguable that in general, (and except in the most serious cases of violence and import-ation), socio-economic status factors still play a larger part in drug-related *crime commission* by women than do addictions un-related to those factors; and that the *custodial sentencing* of women is still as much influenced by socio-economic status, racism and gender-deviant factors as by drug-regulation panics.

Is Racism the Key to Increases in the Female Prison Population?

> In June 1996, there were 10,200 people from ethnic minor-ities in Prison Service establishments. Ethnic minorities accounted for 18 per cent of the male prison population and 24 per cent of the female population compared with 6 per cent of the male and female general populations of England and Wales. (Home Office 1997b)

It is important to note that 43 per cent of the women from ethnic minorities were foreign nationals (not normally resident in England and Wales), primarily in prison for the importation of illegal drugs, and skewing the daily average figures by their longer-than-average sentences. Even so, the official statistics still reveal that 16 per cent of all British nationals in prison in June 1995 were from ethnic minority groups:

> 84 per cent were white; 13 per cent were black; 1 per cent were of Chinese or other ethnic appearance. This compares with the general female population of England and Wales (British nationals aged 15–64) of whom 95 per cent were white, 2 per cent were black, 2 per cent were South Asian and 1 per cent were Chinese. (Home Office 1997b:10)

Leaving aside the questions of general punitiveness against foreign nationals as Northern nations continue to wage 'war on drugs' (see Stanley 1996:122), and that poverty is the reason most frequently given by drug couriers for their crimes (Abernethy and Hammond 1996:136), the statistics also reveal that the proportions of black women in prison have remained much the same throughout the 1990s. It can therefore be con-cluded that the increases in the female prison population relate primarily to an increase in punitiveness toward all women, but with poor women, those with histories of local authority care, and mothers living outwith male-related domesticity continuing to figure disproportionately in the total numbers of women in custody. In such a discriminatory penal culture, black women are more at risk of imprisonment because, as a result of discrimination in employment and welfare control they are more likely to have spent some time in local authority care and more likely to have spent some period of their lives in poverty (see Carlen 1988).

Can it Still be Argued That Women go to Prison Primarily Because They are Destitute and Defined as Gender-Deviant?

It has been well established in recent years that the courts respond to men's and women's crimes differently. Statistical approaches to the question of whether the criminal justice system is more or less punitive towards females than to males can be misleading, and explain little about the size and composition of the female prison population unless it is understood how, in judicial investigations and the sentencing process, demographic factors such as class, race, family status and mental health are encoded with gender stereotypes of how women should behave and be controlled. These stereotypes of permissible and impermissible femininities allow some (usually middle-class white) women, on the one hand 'to get away with murder' (see Allen 1987), while being, in part, responsible for sending other women (usually the destitute, the mentally ill and/or those perceived to be deviant – either sexually or in their family relationships) to prison for crimes like not paying a taxi fare or stealing a pint of milk (see Chapter 1 of this book, and Carlen, 1983 and 1988). Other factors, such as geographical location and the narrow range of penal facilities for women, are also known to influence sentencing decisions in a gender-specific way which disadvantages women again (Home Office 1992b:19). Thus, although in absolute terms, sentences for most women seem usually to be lighter than those for men (Home Office 1992b), when length and type of criminal career are analysed it can be seen that *certain* women, (especially those seen to be outwith the controls of post-school education, the labour market and white British male-related domesticity), are likely to receive more severe sentences than their male conterparts. Furthermore, when women are being considered for a tougher

rather than a milder sentence, they may be escalated up the
tariff towards the custodial end more quickly than a male
purely because the range of non-custodial facilities for women
is narrower – see Chapter 1 of this book, and Carlen 1990).
However, once we turn to remand (as opposed to sentenced)
prisoners it is difficult to think of any explanation for the extra-
ordinary remand statistic that:

> [A]bout 47 per cent of male prisoners received on remand
> were subsequently received with a custodial sentence in 1995;
> for females the proportion was 34 per cent...(Home Office
> 1996b:34)

other than one which concludes that the courts are discriminating against women by irresponsibly using custodial remands
purely for punitive purposes *in cases where they would not use them
for men.* (See Cavadino 1997 for the latest research on gender
differences in Pre-Sentence and Social Inquiry Reports, where
he argues that though recent analyses of SIRs suggest that
there are still gender differences in report emphases, those of
PSRs suggest that gender differences in Report contents are
decreasing.) In sum, then, and despite exaggerated claims
about increasingly violent and addiction-driven female offenders, it appears that there is a consensus amongst analysts and
commentators that the steep increases in the numbers of
women received into British prisons in the 1990s can best be
explained by the increased numbers of women in the social categories of economic need and social deprivation who have traditionally been more vulnerable to imprisonment (Carlen 1988,
1990), and by the increased punitiveness of the courts towards
female offenders in general (Penal Affairs Consortium 1996;
Prison Reform Trust 1996; Fletcher 1997).

PATHWAYS TO THE WOMEN'S PRISONS

Prison officers will often say that in the 1990s a 'different type
of woman is coming into prison'. By this they are usually referring to the women who appear to be in prison purely because of
an 'unfortunate involvement' with drugs – the 'involvement' not
usually being the actual addiction, but more likely an offence
committed to fund a drug habit (not, necessarily the prisoner's

own), or a first-time and out-of-character offence of violence committed under the influence of drink or opiates. Of course, prisons have always contained some middle class people, and the women's prisons continue to receive the 'politicos' whose offences have been carried out in the name of some cause – such as 'animal rights' or 'anti-war', as well as women convicted of the more heinous crimes (eg child murder, child torture) or the serious organized crime that would most probably be viewed as meriting severe punishment in any society. However, these latter still make up only a very small proportion of the total population of the women's gaols, and when prison officers and governors say that they seem to be getting a 'different type' of woman in prison they are usually referring to quiet, competent women like Amanda, (whose story is told below), who just want to get through their sentences without fuss, and who, many probation and prison officers argue, would not have been given a custodial sentence in the 1980s. Nonetheless, although the final stages of individual pathways to the women's prisons may nowadays manifest a greater involvement with drugs than they did earlier in the century, any probe that reaches further back into the histories of women prisoners reveals that: their biographies in general are still disproportionately marked by the myriad misfortunes associated with poverty and damaged childhoods (see HM Chief Inspector of Prisons 1997b); that many of their offences which initially appear to have been precipitated purely by over-indulgence in drugs or alcohol mask psychiatric conditions that should be treated as urgent health problems if the risk of recidivism is to be adequately addressed; and that their careers in the criminal justice system continue to be influenced by gender differences and racist discrimination (Home Office 1992b; Home Office 1995c)

Amanda's Story

Amanda was a 48 year-old lower-middle class woman with no previous convictions who had received a sentence of 2 years 6 months for theft from her employer, the offences having been committed in order to pay off the drug debts of a heroin-addicted son. Prison was not a horrific experience for her. She got on well with officers and other inmates; she was a 'listener' (a prisoner trained and monitored by The Samaritans to listen

to inmates who want someone to unburden themselves to) and
an adviser (to prisoners claiming to have been bullied) on the
anti-bullying scheme. During the five weeks she had been in
Holloway she had worked in Reception. At Drake Hall, where I
talked with her, she was a cook in the staff kitchens. Having
elected to live on a drug-free house, so as to 'avoid the hassle' of
youngsters fighting over drugs, Amanda expressed satisfaction
that she was housed with older women whose backgrounds were
more like hers than were those of the younger recidivist
inmates. Indeed, the pressures from her family had been such
that she had initially been very relieved to be in prison:

> I was happy in Holloway. The officers were very supportive,
> very nice. I was glad to be in prison – full stop. It took me
> away from a situation where I was sort of piggy in the middle:
> one son and my husband coming in from one side and saying
> I shouldn't give him the money; and my other son, who's been
> addicted since he was 16, coming in from the other. None of
> them knew what I was really doing – even the son I was doing
> it for. He just assumed I was earning good money.
>
> Taking me away from the situation has made me re-evaluate
> everything. In fact, I'm in here because I'm too blooming soft.
> Most of the women on my house if you ask them their mitigat-
> ing circumstaces are usually all the same – their business was
> going down the pan and they were trying to keep things going.
>
> It may seem strange that I was glad to be in prison, but it
> was a great relief for it all to be over, for me to be somewhere
> where there was no pressure, and the time was just for
> me…It wasn't a horrific experience. But that's because I have
> a supportive family, unlike most of the young girls here who
> have absolutely nothing.
>
> What really opened my eyes were the backgrounds of these
> young girls. They are in abusive situations, they are very
> heavily into drugs, their children are being taken away from
> them and being adopted, and some of them were virtually
> taken straight off the streets – and so young, so young. The
> bit that stood out for me more than anything was their youth.
>
> On the House I'm on we talk a lot, and when we go home we
> will miss it very much, the communication and the comradery
> that we've had with all the women here. And we all say we're
> going to miss it when we go out, because we realize that to talk

is a very important part of our lives. But let's be honest, it's different out there than it is in here. As soon as you get out you have your life to get on with.

But I don't understand why I was sent to prison for two and a half years. What am I costing the country for me to sit here for fifteen months? The girls on my House were saying it's a shame there isn't a split – seven months in prison, seven months in community service. I can appreciate what the public thinks, because I was once one of the public myself; but there are different categories of crimes, aren't there? I'm not going to hurt anybody. Never have done; never will.

Karen's Story

Karen was a white British woman aged 21, and when I met her in 1996 she had just been released from prison, having served five months of a nine month prison sentence for conspiracy to commit fraud. The offence, committed to fund Karen's crack cocaine habit, had occurred five years before. She had no other convictions and believed that her sentence had contained an exemplary element.

I was fifteen, and it started off as a little joke, you know, just going out and doing a few cheques. Then it got to the stage that I was threatened by the ringleader, and I had to work otherwise my family, who own a pub, was in danger. It turned to threats because I was quite good at what I was doing. The judge said, 'I believe that you were the least involved in this conspiracy, I would describe you as nothing but a foot soldier'. But then he went on to say that he found it difficult to believe that I hadn't offended since that time, that having a drug habit was no reason to be doing that crime, and that therefore he sentenced me to nine months in prison.

He just couldn't believe that I hadn't done anything since then – which I hadn't, you know. I'd moved away from the area – up to London – and I'd rehabilitated myself. I had met my boyfriend who is totally drug-free and he made me make a choice. It was: either carry on doing crime and the drugs or be with him. And I made that choice and for five years I really felt good about myself. Then the police phoned and said that they were going to come in and arrest me. I lost my job, but, during

the time the court case was going on, I started going to college.
So I'd really rehabilitated my life and he still sent me to prison.

Sandra's Story

Sandra, aged 28, was from Jamaica and had been sentenced to
six and a half years for importation of an illegal drug. She had
no previous convictions. I asked her if, being a foreign national,
she had received any special help when she went into Holloway.

No, not much, because the only people we could really speak
to was people who came from Hibiscus or other black worker
schemes.

I had it very hard before I could really get a phone call to
my little boy, because when I told them I wanted to call home
I didn't get no call back to my country until after I was sentenced, and that's after I came here [Winchester]. The only
way I could call home was if I bought the cards myself, and,
having no private cash or anything, I had to save my wages
for a couple of weeks to buy the phone cards.

When I left [Jamaica), my child was on holiday and he was
supposed to go to school the week after I came to England. But
he didn't go to school for all the last year and most of this year
because I'm not out there to pay his school fee. He's with my
brother now, but my brother is not working and has just got to
depend on money that he gets from his mother. It's hard.

I've been on my own since I was 17. I've always been on my
own and I was the main support for my family. At the
moment they can't help me in any way, and I can't help them.

I don't see any necessity of keeping a foreigner in gaol in a
foreign country. I had only 96 grammes and I won't get to see
my son until I get out. We [foreign nationals] don't get town
visits, don't get home leave, don't get nothing. It's hard to get
all the type of products we need for our body. They don't have
a proper understanding of what an Afro body is like, what
your hair is, skin, everything. Even when they do get them
they're expensive. [See Cheney 1993 for comments on the
plight of all foreign prisoners in British gaols]

Back home I've lost everything. I've been working since I
was seventeen, and I didn't get what I had from drugs. I
worked really hard and I've lost everything. I will have

nothing when I go home and I will have to start from zero again, from scratch, as if I'm just leaving my parents' house.

I did it to get money. I was born in a poor family and all the time I've been struggling for this, struggling for that. I mean, if someone comes and offers you something that looks good you're going to take it. If you're poor in Jamaica, even if you've got land, you're still poor because you don't have the amount of funds to live your everyday life. Even if you're working, sometimes the pay you're getting cannot pay the bills. Things there are expensive. The most we think about is to buy a home, and to own a home in Jamaica is a lot of money, because foreigners are coming to buy our land, houses and stuff, and everything just goes up.

Most people live in rented accommodation because you have the rich people come and buy houses and rent them out; you're not working, or, even if you are, you can't pay that amount of rent. It's just survival really. There is no welfare, you've just got to survive on your own.

Amanda, Karen and Sandra are good examples of the range of involvements with drugs that may pave the various, and always varying, pathways to the women's prisons; and of the kind of prisoner who is obviously no threat to the public. Yet, it could be argued, also, that it is to the poverty-stricken women who already have absolutely nothing that prison is so damaging, and whose stories not only suggest that prison does *not* work (in the sense of turning people away from crime) but also confirm that prison, more often than not, makes already-bad social situations worse. There is abundant evidence to show that this is so for both destitute drug couriers (like Sandra) from Third World countries (see Green 1996) and for young women who (like Kitty and Jasmine below) have spent all (or some) of their childhoods and adolescence in state care (see Carlen *et al.* 1985; Carlen 1987, 1988; Carlen and Wardhaugh 1991; Carrington 1993 and Devlin 1998).

Kitty's Story

Kitty was a white British woman aged 41 serving her sixteenth prison sentence for fraud. She had been taken into local authority care at the age of four and had spent three of her teenage years in an approved school. She had three children, two of whom had been treated for severe mental disorders, and she herself had been referred to a psychiatrist on more than one occasion. When I asked her if she had ever been in care, she replied, 'Yes, all my life'.

I was out of parental control at thirteen and they sentenced me to three years in an approved school. In them days, when I went to Risley at thirteen, you'd have to have an internal, you'd have to put your legs in stirrups. As I was a virgin still, that was unreal. So I would say that I was [officially and institutionally] abused in there as well. Then I was sent back to the remand home. I was raped by another inmate but the officers wouldn't believe me. They just put me down the block and put the needle in me – Largactl – and that was it. I'd just turned 17 when I had our James, and then I had Charles in prison.

I never touched drugs, I don't believe in pills. I just wanted to survive, really. So I started doing the social security books and I've done them ever since, from 16 up. One judge said that I'd had an appalling childhood and needed counselling, it was a cry for help, and all that. And then he gives me three years in prison!

I had to survive on my own, because I had no mum and dad there for me. I had foster parents and this, that and the other, and after that it was just prisons, prisons, prisons.

The offences of recidivist ex-care youngsters caught up in the small-time crime incidental to transient lifestyles are usually much more varied than Kitty's. Nonetheless, apart from her rather single-minded career as a petty fraudster, and her abhorrence of drugs, Kitty's story is typical of that of the 30–40 per cent of women prisoners who have spent some time in care. (Figures vary – see Home Office 1992a and HM Chief Inspector of Prisons 1997b. Only about 2 per cent of the general population have been in state care so, given that the foreign nationals could not have spent any time in care in Britain, the number of prisoners who have previously been in care is even more disproportionate than it might seem at first sight.)

In middle age, Kitty appeared to be serving her current sentence more calmly than she had some earlier sentences. As a frightened teenager and stroppy recidivist, with no-one on the outside to care about her, and with nothing to lose either, she had previously spent days and weeks of each sentence in solitary confinement in the punishment cells.

> In those days, I wouldn't be seen dead talking to an officer or anything. I wouldn't even look at one, or if I looked at one, I'd end up fighting them. They'd just put a needle in me and that was it. I was down the block more times than anywhere else.(Kitty, aged 32)

Jasmine's Story

Jasmine was a black woman who, as well as experiencing deprivations similar to Kitty's, also believed that she had been harrassed by racist police officers.

> I was in care from the age of 11, and I came out of care when I was 16 or 17. I was sexually abused at home, so I didn't want to go back home. My mother and father had separated. My mother had a boyfriend and she was going to work in the nights; and he was helping himself to us while she was away. I just couldn't take any more of it, so I left, got myself into trouble with the police outside and ended up in care. When I left care, social services got me my apartment where I was living and I got married.
>
> Then my husband began to take cocaine and started to beat me up. I went to a battered wives' home and from there they put me in a bed and breakfast, and I moved from the flat where I was staying before and ended up in the flat where I am now.
>
> I've never been in prison before, and I don't think I should be here. It's just that the police kept bothering me because I just like ghetto life where they sell drugs and things. I just like hanging around places like that. The police kept picking me up, thinking that I'm selling drugs, carrying me to the station and searching me. They don't find anything on me. So they sent a plain clothes policeman to me (which I didn't know it was a plain clothed policeman), and I went and got it for him from someone else. All this showed on the camera, and I still got four years, despite I pleaded guilty without my solicitor being there. (Jasmine, aged 34)

Jasmine had family and flat to return to when she left prison, and in this she was quite unusual. Twenty of the 39 women interviewed had lost their accommodation while in prison and expected to be homeless upon release.

Sadly, at the end of the century, as in previous eras, it is still the younger women with nothing on the outside who cause most trouble in prison – a not surprising state of affairs as criminal justice personnel themselves are amongst the first to argue. For instance, in 1991, the Probation Inspectorate reported that two women probation officers had made the following comments about a couple of their female clients, and I have heard similar remarks from police, probation and prison personnel who repeatedly come into contact with some of the more troubled young women in the system, and who feel that 'we' should be able to do better than merely bang 'them' up – again, and again and again.

> I don't think I will ever forget one girl we had, the tattoes on her arms and thighs were so lurid that one could not help but wonder what messages she carried on those parts of her body which were not open to the gaze of the likes of me. If I felt that, I wonder what effect she had on the police and the courts! Whenever she was picked up for possession of drugs or soliciting it was straight down or a heavy fine which meant the same thing. But it was help with her self mutilation and drug addiction that she needed, not a spell in the nick.

> She's been utterly abused, physically, sexually and mentally, for most of her life and now she's crushed and embittered and anti-authority; small wonder that when someone in uniform tries to tell her what to do she hits out. We (the Probation Service) offer the best hope of doing something with her but I doubt if we will get the chance, the system can't understand a woman behaving like that, so she will go to prison. (HM Inspectorate of Probation 1991:26)

What kind of a 'system' is it, then, that cannot understand 'a woman behaving like that'? To shed some light on that most silent and complex of systems, it may be instructive to look at the subtle ways in which most women are so effectively and informally regulated, by social (and anti-social) control mechanisms in society at large, that comparatively few ever pass through the criminal courts, let alone the prisons. (As a consequence, the few who do receive custodial sentences, enter a system made for, run by, and primarily geared to, men.)

GENDER, SOCIAL REGULATION AND ANTI-SOCIAL CONTROL

In this book I am using the term 'social regulation' to refer to all the ways in which societies cohere via rule-governed roles and relationships. Under this general term I subsume informal and formal control mechanisms.

'Social control' itself is a vacuous term. Unless closely defined it can imply meanings which range from any type of constraint on individual action; through a 'conspiracy theory' which implies that in 'capitalist', or 'patriarchal' or 'communist' or 'fascist' etc. societies, every social practice is 'really' part of a totalizing 'social control' process – whatever other ends it might appear to serve; to a very narrow conception which refers only to the state's formal apparatuses for crime control and the regulation of other officially-prohibited behaviours. For my purpose here – that of analyzing the different types of 'controls' experienced by women – I shall use the following definitions:

- *Social control* – a generic term for a variety of benign institutionalized practices designed to set limits to individual action in the interests of the collectivity's proclaimed ideals of social and criminal justice as instanced in law and dominant ideologies;
- *Anti-social control* – a generic term for a variety of malign institutionalized practices which may *either* set limits to individual action by favouring one set of citizens at the expense of another so as to subvert equal opportunities ideologies in relation to gender, race and class (or other social groupings); or (in societies without equal opportunities ideologies) set limits to individual action in ways which are anti-social because they atrophy an individual's social contribution and do so on the grounds of either biological attributes or exploitative social relations.

The advantage of these formal definitions when analyzing the main modes of controlling women both within social and criminal justice systems and in society at large is at least threefold. First,

they help avoid libertarian implications that all 'social control' is
'a bad thing'. Secondly, they help avoid the circularity of conspir-
acy-type theories which imply that as a majority of legal and
other state bureaucracies have traditionally been dominated by
men, *all* laws, rules and organizational practices must necessarily
be always and already in the interests of men and against those
of women (for a critique of this position see Cousins, 1980). And
thirdly, they allow the same substantive practices to be theorized
differently according to the differing combinations of economic,
ideological and political conditions in which they are realized.
Thus, for instance, (and to illustrate all three foregoing points in
a way that is very pertinent to our topic here), the contemporary
ideology of child-centredness encapsulated in the phrase 'good
parenting' might be seen as a positively benign form of social
control when actualized in a society where all have equal opportunities and responsibilities to be 'good parents'. But it may
equally be seen as being a very anti-social form of control in societies where some parents are always-already prevented from
being 'good parents' by their adverse economic circumstances; or
in societies where responsibility for 'good parenting' falls systematically upon mothers rather than fathers (or vice versa). In the
former example, 'good parenting' ideology may be seen as being
a form of anti-social control because it includes under its 'ideal'
rule those who are in fact excluded from it by their 'real' circumstances; in the latter example, it may be construed as being an
anti-social control because it subverts a society's equal opportunities rhetoric. In conventional criminological terms, of course, the
'anomie' experienced by those concomitantly included under a
rule and excluded from the conditions necessary to its fulfilment
is a frequent precursor (if not cause) of crime; and the poverty-
stricken women who have perennially justified their stealing or
soliciting by claiming that 'it was only done to feed my kids' are
usually seen to have a point (though not one strong enough to
absolve them from guilt and its subsequent punishment).

Recognition of the salience of informal anti-social is not only
relevant to an understanding of gender differences in the prison
experiences of men and women. It may also be relevant to
explaining the 1990s rise in the female prison population. For if
Feeley and Little (1991) were right in suggesting that the relatively small proportions of women in prison in most Western
countries came about as the informal controls on women were

strengthened and tightened, then it might also be arguable that some of the increases in the women's prison population are attributable to sentencers' perceptions that, as a result of changing family forms (especially as instanced by increases in single parenthood), there has, in the last couple of decades of the twentieth century, been a relaxation of the informal social controls on women, thus making it necessary to redress the perceived imbalance of regulation between males and females by responding to women more harshly whenever they appear in the criminal courts.

WOMEN: IN AND OUT OF CONTROL

As the twentieth century has drawn to its end, there has been a more sustained focus upon the control of women by formal and informal means than there was prior to the mid-1980s. (For a comparative perspective on the search for a feminist jurisprudence see Boyle *et al.* 1985 for Canada; Dahl 1987 for Norway; MacKinnon 1987; and Fineman and Thomadsen 1991 for the United States; Redcar, 1990 and Grbich, 1991 for Australia; and Smart, 1989 for England.) Dominant constructs informing analyses of the major informal modes for regulating women have been those relating to: discursive, ideological and physical control via the politico-economic institutions of family, marriage and welfare; physical and ideological control via the economic systems of capitalism and the structures of patriarchy; and physical and ideological control via the discourses of femininity and the menacing effects of masculinist discourses.

In overviewing the different dimensions of the anti-social control of women I shall be arguing that they all emanate from one fundamental mechanism for keeping women 'in their place': the fracturing of women's subjectivities within complex and contradictory discourses which insist on women's essential 'power for good' (femininity) at the same time as engendering social relationships wherein discourses of femininity are incorporated into masculinist discourses (see, for example, Brittan 1989:4) justifying a close ideological and physical control of women's biological, emotional and intellectual powers. Anne Worrall has described the anguish of being always and already Other.

Women...are always-already *not men*. Femininity is con-
structed on the site vacated by masculinity, and this absence
of maleness is manifested in two opposing sets of expectations (Eichenbaum and Orbach 1983). On the one hand, femininity is characterised by self-control and independence.
Being a normal woman means coping, caring... On the other
hand, femininity is characterised by lack of control and
dependence. Being a normal woman means needing protection (Hutter and Williams 1981). It means being childlike,
incapable, fragile and capricious... [T]he centrality to the
construction of femininity of the dilemma of having to be
both 'in control' and 'out of control' poses a routine
problem.... (Carlen and Worrall 1987:3,8; cf Chesler 1974;
Allen 1987)

For women, then, the Kafkaesque ante-rooms of the criminal
courts are to be found in the simultaneity of the inclusionary
and exclusionary devices of the anti-social family, the anti-social
state, and the anti-social practices and discourses of men's violence, mens rea, men's rule and male menace. Given the
strength and elasticity of these informal controls, the criminal
justice system has seldom to be invoked against women. As a
consequence, when women are on trial, the courts are doubly
punitive towards those whose very presence in court suggests
that they have eluded or violated informal gender controls.
Increasingly, therefore, theorists have focused on these informal controls when analyzing the (anti) social control of women.
It is to three dimensions of these antecedent controls – family,
contradictory ideologies of female citizenship, and competing
masculinities – that we will now turn. Then, in the final section
of the chapter it will be seen how, within the women's prisons,
the further perversion of these already contradictory control
mechanisms gives another painful twist to the penal screw.

Women: In and Out of the Anti-Social Family

The strength of the best studies analyzing the social control of
white, western women within the politico-economic institution
of the family lies first in their historical specificity (even
though, alas, their *cultural* specificity is too often glossed over).
Secondly, it inheres in a thoroughgoing materialism which, in

prioritizing analyzes of the social conditions in which women's physical and economic control is accomplished, is, at the same time, also able to facilitate explanation of the modes of control wherein their *subjective* coercion is achieved. A good example of this type of study is that of Ehrenreich and English which was published in 1979 and entitled *For Her Own Good*. Subtitled '150 Years of the Experts' Advice to Women', the book shows how nineteenth and early twentieth century experts controlled women (and taught middle class 'ladies' how to control working class 'housewives') via an attractive mix of rationalist and romanticist discourses which both objectified women's sexuality in the service of men, and denied them their independence for the 'good of the family'. (See Smart 1992 for a collection of feminist historical essays on the regulation of marriage, motherhood and sexuality.) As Zedner (1991:14), also writing on women in Victorian England, has stressed,

> although women gained considerable power within the limited sphere of their influence, in order to protect their own purity they were admonished to leave the house as little as possible.

The woman 'simply by being a model of chastity, altruism and morality was supposed to induce men to raise themselves to her level of virtue' (Zedner 1991:17–18). While discriminatory laws relating to public life, education and the professions combined to keep middle class women in their place (see Sachs and Wilson 1978), the inter-related institutions of marriage, wage-labour and prostitution kept working-class wives and daughters in theirs. For, though poverty-stricken women might have reason enough to be oft-tempted to rebel against man or master, they had equal reason to fear that no destiny other than prostitution would be the fate of anyone foolhardy enough to risk being cast out 'characterless' by either husband or employer. Thus, historically, women have been expected to subject themselves first, and perennially to the family – in obedience to the rhetoric that 'good mothers make good families make good societies'. Then, contradictorily but simultaneously, they have been expected to accept, and be regulated by, an alternative but equally powerful ideology – that the family itself must forever be at the service of the Military, the Markets and the Man,

Women: In and Out of Female Citizenship

But did women ever have so much power within the home? If one examines closely the public/private distinction ('public' referring to the worlds of work, war and state; 'private' to those of family, intimate relationships etc.) it is easy to establish that the 'privacy of the home' ideology has functioned primarily to allow all kinds of physical and sexual abuses to proceed unchecked on the patriarchal assumption that a 'man's home is his castle'. Moreover, even when domestic violence has not been lacerating families from within, war and poverty have been routinely destroying them from without. British women have twice this century been called upon to encourage their men to go to war, and to leave their children in order that they themselves might go out to work for the war machine. The wars over, women have then been required to give up their jobs to the men, being reminded that their first priority is of course with their children once more – until the next time (Woolf 1991: 161–163 – first published 1938)! However, by the end of the 1940s, it was already being realized that regular war and poverty cycles might no longer be depended upon to discipline families sufficiently to meet the needs of markets. So, the agents of state welfare control made their debuts. Physically, they policed the homes of the poor via their social workers (Wilson 1977). Ideologically, they interpellated mothers of all classes via the 'psy' and 'expert' pedagogies of 'good parenting' and 'child centred familiness' (Donzelot 1979; Meyer 1977; Hall *et al.* 1978; Rose, 1989). Nowadays, women who either cannot or will not pay obeisance to *all* of these opposed ideologies (women who, as one might put it more figuratively, refuse to keep so many balls in the air at once) are likely to be made examples of – by the media, by welfare regulation, or by the courts. Two striking examples from the last decade have been the Greenham Common (anti-war) women; and, most recently, unmarried mothers on welfare.

The founding of the women's anti-cruise missile camp at Greenham Common in 1981 started a women's movement for peace which achieved worldwide acclaim. Its members braved hard weather conditions, separation from families and friends, media derision, arrest, and in some cases, imprisonment. And for over a decade 'they were vilified by some of the British tabloids – as dirty lesbians, soviet stooges, [and] irresponsible wives and mothers' (Coote and Campbell 1987:50). In the long tradition of punitive obloquy directed at women who attempt to link feminism and pacifism:

> The women of Greenham Common came in for a particularly nasty brand of misogynist reporting, which characterised them as dirty violent scroungers who were probably in the pay of Moscow. Worse still, the homophobic press invariabley described them as lesbians in such a way as to denigrate all lesbians, and by association all Greenham women (Coote and Campbell 1987:280).

The media's pillorying of unmarried mothers on welfare has, in the 1990s, been sparked off both by the work of conservative American 'underclass' theorist Charles Murray (1984: 1990) and by a British media-inspired scare about persistent young criminals. Murray's interlinking of 'welfare dependency', single parenthood, undisciplined children and crime in an unbroken causal chain coincides with two other 1990s' concerns; with real doubts about the actual success and future redistributionist potential of western welfare systems; and (in Britain at least) with a conservative backlash against feminist struggles for increased female dependence from male-related domesticity. The imagery used by Murray and other 'underclass' theorists is one of disease and infection, a continuation of a long tradition in which misogyny has combined with exploitative class relationships to ensure that 'undeserving' poor women have been represented both in life and literature as being especially invidious bearers of social and moral contagion. On the war fronts they have been stigmatized as venereally-diseased prostitutes weakening the physical strength of the British army. In the property stakes, they have (like Dumas's *Lady of the Camellias*) been represented as sexual adventurers threatening class structures by bringing the contagion of the gutter right into the heart of bourgeois society. Murray's solution to 'his' problem would involve a 'ghettoization' of 'underclass' families into separate neighbourhoods. Governmental responses to increases in single parenthood have included increased regulation of women on welfare (see Cook 1988) and, more recently, threats to develop new policies to 'deter' women from choosing to rear children apart from men.

Greenham women took seriously the social values of protecting and nurturing children by rejecting militarism. Single mothers on welfare take seriously their duties to their children – but without embracing male-related domesticity and thereby testing the limits to welfarism in an increasingly illiberal welfare state. For their pains (and for opposing militarism and bucking market morality) they are repeatedly subject to exclusionary and anti-social control measures, antecedent to their regulation (or not) by more formal measures.

Women: In and Out of Men's Violence, Men's Rule, Male Menace and Other Anti-Social Masculisms

The anti-social regulation of women has always been as much physical as ideological. Physical exclusion from public space, public institutions and workplaces has primarily been managed via law, economy and tradition. Sexual and physical regulation within the home and on the streets has been via either threatened or actual male violence and the peculiar mix of gender ideologies which engender such violence and facilitate its persistence (Adler 1987; Dobash and Dobash 1979; Dworkin 1981; Radford and Russell 1992). Additionally, in the second half of the twentieth century, a further subjection of women has been achieved: by harnessing media and markets in a double targeting of women's bodies as new sites of anxiety and guilt – about body weight, personal appearance and sexuality (Coward 1984; McRobbie 1991). For women unable to cope, there have been the (overprescribed) tranquillizers (Iles 1986) and the (oversubscribed) mental hospitals (Chesler 1974; Sim 1990). When men and women have been locked in courtroom battles, again and again the judicial concept of *mens rea* has operated only to reflect an empiricist rationality based on men's worldly experiences, not women's (see Chapter 4). This point was well made by an older, male prison officer whom I interviewed and who, having only recently begun working in a women's prison, had been appalled to find how inappropriately geared to men the women's regime was.

The trouble with the criminal justice system is it's been devised by men for men. And somewhere along the line somebody has said, 'Hey, you know, women commit offences

as well'. So OK we'll throw women in the pot'. (Prison Officer
13 – male)

The British criminal justice and penal systems are insemi-
nated by a narcissistic masculinism which, in denoting crime a
male preserve, finds it very difficult to know how to think
about women who, in breaking the law, have dared to be other
than Other (see Allen 1987; Worrall 1990). As a result, women
prisoners have been subjected to fragmented and contradictory policies which have attempted self-justification by alter-
nately invoking either an infantilizing paternalism ('women
prisoners are different to men, they need treatment rather
than punishment'); or a formal – but unsubstantiated – equality ('women and men are equal, therefore male and female
prisoners should be subject to the same prison rules'). Both
perspectives have ignored the most important difference
between male and female prisoners: that 'women-as-a-group'
commit their crimes within material and ideological conditions which are very different to those of men-as-a-group'
(Messerschmidt, 1986). As a consequence of one of those ideologies – that crime is a proof and prerogative of masculinity –
women in prison are not only interpellated as being guilty of
breaking the law, they are also made to feel even more guilty
about being in prison. Accordingly, they take a much heavier
load of 'baggage' with them into prison than men do, and this
'baggage' is comprised (variously) of a compound of anxieties
about the well-being of their families, and questions about
their own self-identities.

GENDER AND PUNISHMENT

To illustrate how the contradictory and ideological control
mechanisms of family, state and masculinism (which frequently
tear women apart outside prison) become entwined with, inflate
and aggravate, women's pain inside (and after) prison, we turn
now to an analysis of the ways in which female prisoners are
caught up and played upon by a web of socio-penal contradictions which call upon them: to relate and not relate to their
families; to relate and not relate to their identities as women;
and to relate and not relate to their bodies

Women, Family and Penal Pain

Whenever I asked people working in the women's gaols if they
thought that women had a different experience of prison to
men, they first mentioned women's special role in the family
both in terms of function and ideology. Usually they illustrated
their remarks by referring only to women as mothers, though
sometimes they would go on to refer to women as more general
carers (of other family members) and to the special dependency
which many men exhibit in relation to their female partners.

Having worked in men's gaols previously, the male staff
presently working in women's prisons spoke with special authority when they compared the ways in which family relationships
and ideologies impact on women's and men's prison experiences. Unsentimentally, and with sociological insight, the
officers recognized that a powerful mix of biological ties, emotional bonds and family ideologies can affect a woman's prison
experience independently of the quality of her performance as
a mother prior to imprisonment.

> I've had twenty years of males, and in 99 per cent of cases,
> when a man comes into prison and he's got a home and
> family, he comes in with the certain knowledge that those
> kids are being looked after by the wife or whatever, and that
> the DSS is paying the rent. When the females come in, it's
> quite often the case that if they are attached to a male, he is
> in the prison system somewhere anyhow, so, of course, then
> they're losing their houses, and quite often they're losing the
> children to foster care. (Governor No 6 – male)

> Because they are closer to the children and the home,
> females lose far more when they come into prison than male
> prisoners do. The females have a closer bond with their chil-
> dren and it affects them far more. When males come to
> prison, the wife's at home looking after the children;
> whereas, when women come in, quite often the husband's not
> there or not capable of looking after a kid. So social services
> become involved, probation becomes involved.

> When a woman is in prison, far more pressure is put on
> her by the spouse, than a female spouse will put on a male
> prisoner. The greatest worry with male inmates is, 'What's
> she getting up to while I'm inside?' whereas women are more

concerned about domestic things, the house, the family, the child's education, 'what am I going to do when I get out?' sort of thing. (Prison Officer 16 – male)

When a woman goes to prison she still manages the family. The male partner very often dumps the kids with somebody else, or into care, and goes off with the blonde down the road. Whereas, when a man goes to prison, the female partner looks after the kids, hauls the children all over the country for a visit, and so forth. One of the things which struck me about visits when I came here, [women's prison], was the way in which the women would get all dressed up for the partner who was expected, and then he wouldn't come. She would be lucky if she got a phone call to say, 'Sorry, love, there was a dart match, or football match', or 'I was under the car', whatever, 'See you next week'. To him it was nothing. To her it was the end of the world. (Governor No 4 – male)

Ok, you can say all sorts of things about families, but when the male is locked up, he's locked up by himself and his family is surviving quite well. He's just looking after himself in an all-male environment. When you're locking up a woman, you're doing a different ball game altogether. Very often the woman has been the supporting pillar of the family, no matter how badly she's done it.

She's generally got kids and invariably the husband will be out of work. You'll generally find that when she's in prison he's got a job to manage the family unit, and if there's no kids you'll find that he'll be off with the woman down the road. So, you're doing far more damage to the female that's being locked up – far more damage to the family unit – than you'll ever do to the male. Because there is a difference between locking up men and locking up women. That lass we saw this afternoon: she's a lousy mother – I've no problem in saying that because I know her history – she's a bloody awful mother. But she carries her photographs of them kids around and she's still distraught that they're going to be adopted by her brother. Now, there's not many men as would be. The male would be like, 'Er, OK, get rid of them. Next, please.' (Prison Officer 13 – male)

The problems that women have got inside are far greater than men inside because very often the women are left to cope with extended family responsibilities. I mean, men don't go to prison for a rest, but certainly their families are sort of at a distance and their [the men's] needs are expected to be catered for rather than the other way round. I've found men very selfish in that respect, in the demands they place on their families. (Prison Governor No 1 – male; cf Fishman 1990)

Women are very demanding, and, with the baggage they have, a lot more complex. For instance, they'll say: 'I look after my partner's health. If he needs a doctor, I'm the one that rings up the doctor. If he needs a prescription, I'm the one that will go and get it.' Women still worry about that when they're in custody. They literally run their homes from within the prison. For example, there was one in May who used to ring home every morning to make sure everyone was up, to make sure the kids were dressed, to make sure they'd had their breakfast and to make sure they'd gone to school.
  Men go into custody and it's like them having a rest. They've always got somebody outside. If it's not the female partner or the wife, the mother will be doing it or the sister. Men don't carry that excess baggage along with them. (Prison Officer 11 – female)

I had a woman in last week who had run a corner shop, an off-licence with her husband. Her offence had been against her brother, so the family wasn't willing to help her. So the husband was trying to run the corner shop and the off-licence, go to the cash and carry, and look after the children. And wasn't succeeding very well. Also, his English wasn't very good, because she was the one who did the ordering and the paperwork and all that. She was desperately worried about him, so I rang the Probation Office and they eventually sent someone out. When they rang back they said the man had left the children on their own while he went to the cash and carry for things for the shop, so they called in Social Services. He obviously wasn't coping and that was what she had been worrying about. (Probation Officer 2 – male)

The added burden that men don't have is actually to get the children together from the different relatives, or from care, or from lodgings (because even if it's lodgings the landlady will take a single person but not a whole family) – and bring them all back into one home. And a lot of them who billet their children with friends and relatives won't claim the money those relatives are entitled to because they're terrified of being involved with Social Services. (BOV 3)

Several prisoners gave details of how their families had been split up while they were serving their sentence:

I went to court, and I had no arrangement for my children, because I had never been in trouble before. I had a nervous breakdown when I come in, but I had to pull myself together to sort out something about the children. My mother has two of them on the Isle of Wight; my brother-in-law has my son in London; and then the three year old is with her natural father in Birmingham. (Nicki aged 33)

Despite the many comments from prison personnel suggesting that there was a new understanding of women prisoners' special family-related problems, staff and inmates agreed that it was very difficult to deal effectively with family crises while a woman is in prison. Rather, it was claimed, the additional security measures brought into play in the 1990s had made keeping in contact with families much more difficult (see Chapter 3). Some prisoners went further, and insisted that there was an institutionalized indifference to family problems:

My little boy had a kidney operation when he was a baby, so he was on lots of drugs for a while. When he went to my Mum on the Isle of Wight, they wanted to know his medical history, and she phoned the prison, but they wouldn't let me speak to her. So she phoned Probation and I had to do it through her. I found the prison really unhelpful with things like that. (Nicki, aged 33)

I knew a girl in there whose children were in foster care, and they were sleeping on the floor. It took her six days to find out what was going on. (I know, because I helped her – she was deaf.) They say, 'We'll do what we can'. But they don't do it that day, they do it three days later. Some girls are suicidal because nobody will help them. Probation, social work don't want to know. But these girls still have problems to cope with in prison. They've got children in homes outside that still need running. You see, Pat, if a man goes to prison, he's still got his wife at home to look after his children, and everything is there. (Kay, aged 46)

The difficulty of getting already overstretched social services to deal with prisoners' problems was confirmed by probation officers working in two of the women's establishments:

> Social workers won't get involved unless they see there's a really desperate case. They don't seem to do any preventative work now. I mean, we had a woman here whose mother was a drinker and was looking after the children. Every so often she would go out on a binge. So we tried to get the social services involved. Well, they visited once and the mother was OK, she wasn't drinking. So they said, 'It's alright', and that they wouldn't come out until there was a real crisis. They were not prepared to monitor and said, 'We're not into that'. When we managed to get them to call when she was actually drinking it was a different matter. Then they did get involved. (Probation Officer 2)

> Social Services will not visit – so disempower the women completely. Prison staff will send down little notes saying, 'Can you see this woman, she doesn't know where her children are'. She's come in, she knows her kids have gone off to aunt or granny initially, she hears on the phone there's been problems: so and so has got the kids; no, so and so has. So dad pops up from somewhere, whizzes off with the kids. Then a lot of our time will be spent contacting Social Services, saying, 'Look, can you find these children?'. And, I have to say that we have to up the ante to get a response. (Probation Officer 4 – female)

And we have to remember that even though staff of the women's prisons are aware of inmates' family difficulties, their awareness has, in most cases, been sharpened by the excess of pain that women suffer directly as a result of: being imprisoned so far from their families – ('It's bad enough being in prison, but being isolated from your family as well! It's a bit much.' Jean, aged 24); the tension that is caused by the restrictions on the number of phone calls allowed – ('We're here [Durham H Wing] long-term and so far away from our families that with not being able to afford the extra phone cards, the relationships with our families are undermined.' Jeanette, aged 37); and the extreme difficulties confronting women dealing with questions of child custody, divorce and family bereavement while in gaol. Finally, although there are mother and baby units, they do not cater for remand prisoners, nor for all sentenced women who are pregnant. An officer at Risley Remand Centre outlined some of the difficulties she was experiencing in 1997:

> A remand centre does not cater for women on remand who are pregnant. If a woman has a baby while she's on remand in custody, social services would be contacted and the baby would be taken off her. She's being denied the right to bond with that baby at such a vital stage. And she's innocent until proved guilty! It causes a lot of distress, because they know from the word 'go' that if they're still on remand the baby will be taken off them.
>
> Another problem that we have is that if they are sentenced we initiate the procedure for applying for a mother and baby unit, but there are not enough Mother and Baby spaces for them to go to.

At Holloway, a personal officer talked of the pain involved in separating a long-term prisoner from the baby that she has borne in prison:

> If you're doing eleven years you're going to have to hand your baby out at eighteen months – even if we can get a place in a mother and baby unit for nine or eighteen months. And then we have to do the separation plan, which is horrible.

Over the past twenty years I have visited many women's prisons – in the United Kingdom, United States, Canada, Australia and New Zealand – and always the one dominant theme has been the intractibility of the prisoners' family problems or desperate social circumstances on the one hand and, on the other, the inappropriateness of prison as a site for addressing either the prisoners' immediate problems or the bureaucracies outside the prisons within which the problems of the poor are, ironically, as frequently inflated and maintained as ameliorated (see Carlen 1996).

> Women prisoners have a lot more problems because of their home and family. As you know, a lot of them lose their homes now because of the housing benefit being cut off at thirteen weeks. A lot of authorities won't pay it at all – even for the thirteen weeks – if they know the woman is going to be away longer than that. They have no obligation. So she loses her

home, she can lose all her furniture, and, of course, she's got anxieties about her children. We had a very stupid case last week where a woman's sister was looking after the children and couldn't get any money from the DSS at all, because they were waiting for child benefit to approve the claim. Once they could get one claim approved, they could get the other, but the child benefit office was slow, and this woman had been waiting six weeks and had had no money. In the end they got the MP involved and he managed to get them to pay the income support without the child benefit...But all the stress caused! Just by that office being so slow...(Probation Officer 2 – male)

Many of the English prison officers who talked with concern about particular prisoners also stressed to me that these were 'ordinary decent women, bringing up families'. Maybe so. Nonetheless, and from a different standpoint, a statistical picture of the women's prison population indicates that women prisoners have been disproportionately victims of family violence, sexual abuse, poverty and mental illness; and disproportionately in local authority care. They may indeed be decent mothers, but in many cases their own family histories will not have been happy ones. A member of a Board of Visitors shook her head in disbelief as she remarked, 'I'm just amazed that, with the enormity and complexity of the problems they have, they remain sane'. A NACRO worker went into greater detail when explaining to me that she counselled women prisoners suffering from stress:

It could be the stress of things happening outside with the family. But when one scratches the surface, the majority of women I see also report episodes of abuse in their childhoods and violent relationships. Generally they are women who have not experienced a great deal of love and care – and they may have been in some form of institution. This is the bread and butter stuff of working with women prisoners. (NACRO 1)

That being so, it seems to me that, while mothers continue to be locked up for relatively minor offences, the official concern about 'families' in the women's prisons is at best nothing more than empathetic collusion in the still-dominant ideological illusion of 'happy familiness'. At its worst, it is either sheer muddled-headedness or institutionalized hypocrisy. For though the 'happy families' myth may approximate to the experience of a significant number of inmates (whose families, as we have seen, are in any case frequently torn apart by their imprisonment), it certainly does not enter the stories of those others who are in prison precisely because the intractibility of their social and personal problems means that no other agency will even attempt to help them (see Carlen 1983; 1988). These are often the women who are extremely difficult whilst in custody and with whom many prison officers, overworked and understaffed as they are, understandably have very little patience. They know from experience that whereas mothers with dependent children will try to do their time quietly and without trouble, previously institutionalized women without families or homes to return to, have little to lose by being violent, taking drugs and generally creating mayhem in the gaols. Moreover, and as we shall see in greater detail in Chapter 3, the mountains of paperwork which increasingly feature in the workloads of prison officers do little to address prisoners' family or other personal problems. Assessments, form-filling, interviews, plans, programmes and therapies may all attempt to create the illusion of a scientific penality, but they also paper-over the most horrendous social problems until such time as the prison can eject a lawbreaker in a much worse material and emotional state than when she came in (see Carlen 1994). In short, although both prisoners' pain and prison officers' control strategies are equally shot through with the ideology of 'happy familiness', the women's prisons can deal effectively with neither the family-related nor the non-family-related problems of women prisoners – as prison staff from three continents have repeatedly stressed to me – and as I was most recently reminded by the ex-governor of an English women's prison in 1997 when he sadly explained:

I always used to feel with men prisoners that they expected that they would get some sort of result when they came and gave you an earbashing about their problems. And there was usually a number of things in your arsenal that you could do for them. Then I went to Holloway and again I walked round in the evenings and listened to them. And I was collared by women with a huge list of problems – most of them to do with the family – none of which there was the slightest hope of doing anything about. And I can remember feeling desperate, knowing I could do absolutely nothing.

And a prison officer put a slightly different gloss on the same issue when she shrugged and said:

> We're called social workers, counsellors, jailers. We're the whole spectrum...and with very little training. (Prison Officer 6 – female)

So there it is. In this section it has been suggested that women's family responsibilities and previous family histories interact (variously) with dominant ideologies about women's place in the family and (contradictorily) with the rigours of state punishment – to increase several-fold the pains of penal incarceration. To make matters even worse, imprisonment can also play havoc with women's sense of self-identity and self-control. Not least because, as you may have already noted, despite the sympathy that many male staff have for their female charges, their comments are still imbued with a masculism which does not get us far beyond the conventional binary perception that 'women are not men'! In Chapter 4 we will try to go beyond this analysis and ask what might be the sentencing and institutional implications of a new women-wise penology.

Female Identity, Pollution and Penal Pain

> 'Space in prison is...both familiar and hostile...' (Davies 1990:59)

> I did not stir, I stood waiting in the middle of the cell, I listened, my ears were filled with the shutting of the cell door: I shall never forget it. I took another step and was up against the cell wall...then I set about measuring the distance between the other two walls, I went back again to the middle of the cell, then to the left up to the wall...this was the cell, they had assigned it to me, and I was busy taking possession of it, taking possession of it. (Bienek 1972, in Davies 1990:61)

> I just couldn't believe it when I opened the door, that I was going to be put in a room like this, with graffiti all over the wall. The room was filthy, the mattresses were filthy. Two of us got moved together, and we literally scrubbed our room from top to bottom. I scrubbed my loo, and it was sparkling in the end. (Amanda, aged 48, talking about Holloway Prison, London, in 1997)

Prisons (as institutions) are, from the perspective of th
oners, essentially about loss of control over personal space.
Erving Goffman (1968) Cohen and Taylor (1972) and Melossi
and Paverini (1981) have vividly illustrated how imprisonment
(as process) is, again from the perspective of prisoners, also
about loss of control over time. As I talked with staff and
inmates of the English women's prisons in 1997, they frequently
ruminated upon the ways in which loss of control over place,
space and time affects women prisoners' sense of self and personal identity differently to the ways in which the same losses
affect men. A variety of illustrations, (some of them applicable
to all women, others either culturally specific or peculiar to the
way English women's prisons are run) were given to support the
argument that imprisonment makes more (or different) inroads
upon a woman's sense of self-identity and self-control than it
does upon a man's. Moreover, though loss of control over physical space and psychic time was a prime concern, complaints
about the loss of female autonomy in prison were never
straightforwardly, or solely, about physical confinement and
temporal drift. They tended to be more complex. Explicitly,
they highlighted how specific features of women's imprisonment deny to prisoners control of those physical and functional
spaces which are in part constitutive of their female identities
outside prison. Implicitly, they indicated how loss of control over
personal space involving physical confinement and disorienta-
tion, psychic coercion, and intimate intrusions into the bodily
regions of the self, can induce in imprisoned women an often
unspeakable, and always corrosive, fear of pollution. (In
Chapter 3 it will be argued that such fears were further aggravated during the 1990s by, amongst other things, the tightening
of both static and dynamic security controls.)

Physical Confinement and Psychic Disorientation

Once you get into prison you have to become an automatum,
ultimately, in order to survive. Have you ever read *Lord of the
Rings?* In it there's something called the Land of Mordor, the
Dark Lord. And there's a magic ring, and whoever has the
magic ring on they can vanish physically, but those who are in
the domain of the Dark Lord, the Vaders, can see you. That's
what the prison system is. You actually have to obliterate

your own self in order to preserve it. But they can see you. (Claire, aged 37)

When people go into prison, they've got to use their heads to block off the outside world, and then they have to live inside there. (Deborah, aged 31)

Intimations of polluted places and spaces (both physical and psychic) usually stem from perceptions either that the conventional spatial and temporal properties and boundaries have been violated, or that there is an inappropriate juxtaposition of objects – with each other and/or with people. This is one reason why space in prison is both 'familiar and hostile'. But control of knowledge in prison is another essential component of the prison's complex of power, and though one form of effective coercion in modern gaols may well emanate from the seemingly transparent assessments, programmes, plans, and timetables of a modernist bureaucratic penality (Foucault 1977), exact knowledge of how the rules will operate for particular prisoners is hidden by a postmodern arbitrariness and individualized coercion which seeks justification by emphasizing that penal justice is indivuated to meet the different needs of different institutions, different prisoners, and an ever-changing penal politics.

Prisoners never know exactly which rules are in operation, when they will be moved from one prison to the next, when they will return to their cells and find that they have been 'turned over' in a cell search, when association will be cancelled for the evening and they will have an extra four or five hours alone in their cells, or when they will be taken for a strip search or a urine test. This may be why so many prisoners told me that in prison they were always aware of a non-specific fear which they found hard to put into words:

The worst thing in prison is fear, no-one helping you, no-one telling you what to do. It's as if they try to take everything away from you, your dignity, everything. I didn't want to give it away, but they pull so much, they take everything, tore my life to bits. (Karen, aged 21)

Prominant amongst illustrations of the more specific fear of pollution and identity crises caused by inappropriate placing and spacing in the women's penal system were examples relating to the narrower range of custodial facilities for women, the humiliating pettiness of many of the rules and the rigidity with which they are enforced, and the erosion of control over the ordering of personal space and time.

Several of the prisoners interviewed indicated that they believed they had been dealt with unjustly. Most thought they should not be in prison at all, either because their offence was relatively trivial, or because it had been their first time in trouble. Others thought that even if they merited a custodial sentence, deprivation of their liberty should be the punishment in itself – they should not also be treated as if they were mentally ill or drug-users (when they had never had any history of either mental illness or drug use), or as if they were children or disturbed young women (when they were stable adults used to running a home and holding down a job). The first complaint related to the increasingly punitive sentencing of women which has already been discussed. The second, about the inappropriateness of the prison regimes, was provoked by their experience of the relatively narrow range of facilities for women which, when stretched by the overcrowding in the women's establishments, results in the women's prisons often having to hold seriously disturbed youngsters or recidivists requiring close supervision alongside prisoners who could be accorded more autonomy. The long-term prisoners in Durham H. Wing had felt this sense of injustice very keenly ever since the Wing had been taking prisoners who had been causing trouble in other gaols:

> Take medication. We used to be allowed it in our possession, mine's HRT, hers is Evening Primrose. But now we all have to line up for it every morning. The trouble is that some people abuse the system by saving up their medication, or swap medication – put themselves at risk, OD or whatever. Then we all have to suffer for it, and that annoys you, when you're sensible. The staff can see the difference between us, but everybody's put in the same category. (Val, aged 50)

A prisoner at Drake Hall expressed similar views:

> It strikes me that this is an adult prison in a young offenders' prison, and I don't think the two mix very well together. We're all treated as young offenders and I do resent being patronized and humiliated by women young enough to be my

daughters. There doesn't seem to be much attention paid to different sentences or people's different needs, even though there are notices up all over Holloway saying that fair treatment doesn't mean the same treatment for all. (Samantha, aged 51)

And Claire well-summarized the irritation that many prisoners expressed about the infantilization which has been exhaustively documented in previous books about the women's prisons (especially in Carlen 1983), but which, none the less still goes on:

I wanted to take control of my life again, but I just couldn't cope with this infantilizing that happens, you know, calling officers 'Miss' and 'Sir'. The system absolutely breaks you up, depersonalizes you. It's as if they create this dependency to service the regulars. But I never called them 'Miss' or 'Sir'. (Claire, aged 37)

In fact there have always been observations that discipline in the women's prisons is more exacting and petty than in the men's. Two explanations are offered. First, that as women prisoners are less violent than males, and as, also, it is in the nature of prisons constantly to stamp their authority upon inmates, in the absence of more serious rule-violations, women prisoners can expect to be punished for relatively venial offences which might be ignored in the men's gaols (cf Durkheim 1964). Yet this Durkheimian approach does not explain why women are regularly charged with proportionately more prison offences than men. So we must look to the second – double barrelled – explanation: that a higher standard of behaviour is expected of women, whether they are in prison or not, and that the knock-on effect of this is that once they are in custody they are defined as being doubly deviant (as citizens and women), and therefore deserving of double punishment. Whatever the explanation, the pettiness of the discipline in the women's prisons has been regularly commented upon by everyone from the Chief Inspector down (see for instance, HM Inspectorate 1994), and it is a major source of frustration, anger and minor outbreaks of trouble (see Carlen 1983; Carlen *et al.* 1985).

There is a negative culture in women's prisons, and much of it is very punitive. (Senior Official in the Home Office)

I was shocked when I came here at the severity of the female staff towards the prisoners, much severer than male staff on male prisoners, much less tolerant. Whether it's because they view women prisoners as having let the sisterhood down, I'm not sure... (Governor No 7 – male)

But what nagged most painfully at the women's sense of injustice was that they often found the rules of open prisons even more restrictive and more closely adhered to than those in closed prisons.

You can be in trouble for walking on the grass, being late for check, locking yourself out of your room – you're booked for all those silly things. (Nicki, aged 33)

They say this is an open prison but the rules they've got here are so petty. Three days for this, three days for that. So, in a way, I would rather do my sentence in a closed prison. (Jean, aged 24)

Finally, all the prisoners (and many of the staff) expressed exasperation at the wide discretion given to Governors about the interpretation of prison rules and regulations – (for further discussion of rule interpretation in a 'blame culture' see Chapter 3):

At Bullwood Hall they allow things that they don't allow at Cookham Wood. So you might be punished for something at Cookham that you were allowed at Bullwood. (NACRO 1)

Everybody does it differently, even though it is written down so clear. At Askham there was an hilarious problem once. You could have three pairs of shoes and a pair of slippers. But did the slippers count as shoes or not? It went on and on, quite a saga. (Prison Officer 12 – female)

Prison officers all have different answers because Brockhill is run different to Holloway, Holloway is run different to Bullwood Hall. The prison officers are from all over the country, and each one tells you a different thing. (Kay, aged 46)

An area of arbitrariness that prisoners found very distressing was in relation to the lack of control over their time in the prison, in particular, the routinely sudden discoveries that they were to forego association by being locked unexpectedly in their

cells, either because of staff shortages or because of another
organizational problem.

> I felt I was going mad when I was locked in the cell. The
> longest period was when a knife went missing out of the
> kitchen, and we were locked up for three days, you know,
> getting fed through the hatch on the door. Luckily I had got
> myself a book, and I was doing meditation, so I got through
> those three days. But I don't know how other people done it.
> (Jill, aged 45)

Young women in the punishment cells can spend much longer
locked up.

The women's heavy responsibilities for families outside,
together with their many-faceted sense of injustice about conditions and regimes inside, may go some way towards explaining
why all staff, both male and female, claimed that women prisoners are more argumentative and less willing to take 'no' for
an answer than males. The staff themselves usually explained
the women's tendency to 'argue about everything' by observing,
first, that women are more prone to relieving frustrations via
talk than violence; and that, secondly, because women are used
to working alone and independently in the domestic and personal presentation spheres, they are more reluctant to yield
autonomy over the minutiae of everyday living to the prison.
(Or words to that effect!):

> It's different for men. If they're fortunate enough, they go to
> work, get into a job and are told what to do. That's it, they're
> conditioned through their working lives to being told what to
> do. And when they go to prison and they're told to scrub a floor,
> they do it. With a woman, once she's had a child and is at
> home, she's a self-governing unit. She makes her own decisions
> – when she has her lunch, when to do the shopping, when to
> have coffee. She makes her own plans for the day. When she
> comes into prison, you can't just seem to say, 'Scrub the floor'.
> She won't refuse, but she'll say, 'I'll do it when I've done so and
> so'. You say, 'No, do it now'…'But I've got other things'…and
> you could spend all day arguing. (Governor No 4)

But there may be more to it than that. For though it is certainly a
contradiction in traditional ideologies about 'woman's place' that
while women have been expected to be strong as mothers and

carers in the so-called private sphere of the family, they have been required to be mild and submissive as citizens in the public sphere, it might well be argued that nowadays, another layer of contradiction is being added – the injunction that women should be more assertive. At the end of the twentieth century it is accepted practice for therapists and teachers to exhort troubled women to bring their emotions to the surface and to be more assertive. (By contrast, in men's prisons therapists are more likely to be teaching aggressive men how to deal with stress without being violent). Problems arise, however, when therapies and teachings about increased assertiveness are brought into the penal sphere, where they can provoke a questioning of the legitimacy of penal discipline. Such questioning is inevitably seen as an undermining of authority towards which prisons, by their very nature, have to be antagonistic. The resulting ironies are not lost upon either therapists or prison personnel:

> The problem with counselling in prison is that you are not in a therapeutic environment. So I can spend an hour and a half with a woman, and she may come from seeing me, and she may well kick-off that night, she may well be throwing things. Then prison officers will say, 'She's been a bloody sight worse since she's been to see you. At least she was quiet before'. So I have to explain to them that she's working through a lot of pain. (NACRO 1 – female)

> Sometimes prison is the first time for them [prisoners] to stop and look where they are in their lives, and it gives them space. The point is, then we have the institutional dilemma of saying to women,'Be assertive, be confident'. And, as soon as they begin to exercise that assertiveness, staff say, 'Whoa! This is a prison, get back there'. And they put them back into an infantile, dependent mode. So there is always this battle and conflict going on. (Governor, No 7 – male)

> There is a conflict of interests. The educationalists identify the need for women to mature, and to have a greater sense of personal worth. And this does make them more – I wouldn't say assertive – more inclined to question, to stand up and look the officer in the eye. And it can cause resentment, because that sort of prisoner is seen as being more difficult to manage than one who is compliant...(Bov 3)

Very closely connected to women prisoners' dislike of the petty rules, infantilization and lack of control over their own body-space and presentation (see below) is their dislike over the more direct psychological attacks on their privacy that are made by officers who expect them at least to 'mix' or 'be sociable' with other prisoners; or, at most, to 'open up' to officers and confide their problems. Rosalie summed up the feelings of several prisoners who desire to keep themselves to themselves in prison:

> Some officers can't handle the fact that I don't mix, and they aren't very nice – to put it politely. I have nothing in common with them, and I have nothing in common with the other girls here, except that I've been found guilty by a jury. And I'm not meaning any disrespect to any of them by saying that. (Rosalie, aged 58)

When it came to confiding in the disciplinary staff, however, some prisoners were less concerned about whether or not they had anything in common with the officers, and more concerned that it was simply inappropriate (emotional pollution?) to have a confidential relationship with someone embodying the all-encompassing powers of a gaoler:

> Confide in someone who can lock you up, strip-search you, watch you urinate and take you down for punishment? It's sick. (Claire, aged 37)

But the dilemma for the prison staff is that many women in prison *do* have multiple personal problems, *do* need some help, *and that prison is simply not the place where such help can be effectively provided.*

> We have people who in my opinion are mentally ill. Yes, they are violent and disruptive, but they're mental. Psychiatrists say they have a personality disorder and they're fed back into the system. It is quite evident, even if you haven't got a medical qualification that they are not well. Over on the health centre you have nursing staff, but its discipline staff that deals directly with them if there's a problem. They do a good job over there, but they're not qualified and if that woman is kept in custody and not getting medical attention she will be released one day back into society with the same problem – only to come back into custody. (Prison Officer 11 – female)

Foreign nationals who understand no English are even more likely to end up in the wrong place, as a member of a Board of Visitors pointed out:

> Recently we've had a lot of Peruvians who could not read Spanish, so you couldn't even give them any information to read. The particular problem is medical issues. They sent one woman to the VD Clinic because she had a problem with her eye – which is terribly insulting – just because nobody spoke her language (BOV 1)

> We've had girls who for religious reasons find it very hard to share a cell. Obviously, if they're getting up in the morning and chanting, it's not very good for their cell mate and that causes a lot of problems. (Prison Officer 17 – female)

Intimate Intrusions
It has already been suggested that women prisoners are engaged in a constant struggle to survive threats to their self-respect which emanate from: the prison's usurpation of their domestic roles; the constant hijacking of any control they might temporarily establish over their living quarters; the infantiliza-tion still inherent in some of the disciplinary regimes in the women's institutions; and the psychic coercion which is a routine feature of the relationship between the gaoled and her gaolers. Yet, anxious as they have always been about the difficulties of maintaining their dignity in face of all these threats to it, the scores of women I have interviewed over the years have expressed even more distress and anger about those aspects of penal power which are exercised most directly upon their bodies. Food, health and hygiene, and institutional sexual abuse (in the form of violations of body privacy and enforced submissions to inspections of body parts normally protected from the public gaze) have perennially been the most fre-quently mentioned causes of concern. The volume and intensity of the complaints about these intimate intrusions have not been diminished by innovations such as integral sanitation, manda-tory drug testing or cross-gender postings, as will be seen in Chapter 3.

Prison food featured prominently in discussions of women's special problems in prison.

> At Holloway the food was horrible. I bought most of my food
> from the canteen because I found a cockroach in my rice that
> had obviously been cooked with the rice, and I couldn't
> handle that. (Karen, aged 21)

Overall, however, the criticisms were not so much about the
quality of the food. Rather the main argument was that as
women's relationship to food outside prison is so different to
men's it is not surprising that their loss of control over its pur-
chase, preparation and presentation in gaol can both affect
their self-esteem – in relation to loss of function – and cause
them much anxiety – in relation to health, diet and body
shape.

> Whereas men generally tend to eat what's put in front of
> them, women don't. And of course, the other bit is that they
> get quite resentful about the fact that if they were given the
> rations to cook with they could produce a much better quality
> meal. (Governor No 2 – female)

> A woman told me an interesting story. She had a weekend
> leave [at home with her husband and son] and she said
> Friday night they all had a take away, and Saturday they went
> somewhere. On the Sunday, it was about 12 o'clock, her son
> said to her, 'Mum, what about lunch?' And she said she just
> sat and looked at him. She said, 'I had completely forgotten
> what you had to do to make lunch – and I'd only been in six
> months'. I think that prison completely disables a woman,
> and yet we're supposed to be preparing them to go out. It's
> the nature of prison, to be totally disabling. How do you get a
> non-disabling set-up? Well, to begin with, I do think that
> taking control of your food would be important. (BOV 1)

> Women often don't want the same dietary provisions as
> men. The food is far too stodgy, and if, on top of that,
> they're not getting any physical activity many of them are
> concerned about their weight. It's all self-image. If you're
> feeling particularly low, often one of the things you try to do
> is to maintain your own physical appearance as a way of
> combating the low self-esteem that you feel. [In women's
> prisons sharing a site with a male prison] it's one central
> kitchen and you therefore have to cook the same for every-
> body. Whereas the women would be more than happy with

salads and sandwiches, rather than having three cooked meals in a day, three cooked meals is what they get. And obviously quite high in calories. It may seem a quite trivial thing to people who're not in custody, but meals are actually quite a milestone in the day in prison. (Gov No 2)

What you are looking at is a lot of carbohydrate, a lot of starch. Things like meat pies and chips, day in, day out. No fresh fruit, maybe an apple once a week (NACRO 1)

I must say that there is no low fat diet at all. I asked for a low chloresterol diet and was told that quiche and chicken pie were low fat diets. We don't have fresh vegetables apart from carrots, and there is very little fruit – maybe an apple or pear twice a week. (Kay, aged 46)

We don't get enough fruit, for definite. Look at me. I'm a prime example: pale skin, rashes from the soap powder. Typical gaol look. (Liz, aged 19)

I asked for skimmed milk – I have been told to have it because of my heart condition. I got it in the end, but it took weeks – and they don't like you to push. (Rosalie, aged 57)

My front teeth have started decaying and I think it is because we are not getting enough nutrients in the food. Breakfast is just corn flakes and milk, every day we have chips with maybe a burger or something like that. Just mostly carbohydrates with no form of protein. I find a lot of changes in my body – spots and stuff coming out on our faces and bodies because of the type of food that is going into our systems. (Sandra, aged 28)

Health and hygiene is a continuing issue in women's prisons (see Sim 1990; HM Chief Inspector of Prisons 1997b). In the country at large, women, especially mothers, are targeted by health campaigners, advertisers and educationalists as being the main guardians of the country's physical, mental and emotional well-being. Whether or not women outside prison heed the injunctions to lead a healthy life, it is arguable that, because of the ways they are interpellated as guardians of health and home-hygiene, women in prison are much more conscious of health hazards than male prisoners are. Not only that. The differential dietary needs of women prisoners has been acknowledged since the beginning of the century at least. A

1922 Report edited by Stephen Hobhouse and Fenner Brockway commented:

> In prisons which contain both men and women prisoners it is customary for the cooking to be done on the men's side and the food sent over to the women's, an arrangement which does not conduce to its being served hot... The diet of women prisoners scarcely differs from that of the men...the interval of over 14 hours ...between the last meal at night and the first in the morning appears to be felt even more by the women prisoners than by the men. (Hobhouse and Brockway 1922:342 and 344)

A regular complaint from women in some prisons is that they have to eat their food in their cells, sitting on their beds – in close proximity to the flush lavatory or a pot. Some also complained about their restricted access to fresh water.

> Sometimes you're allowed out for your meal, but sometimes you're not even allowed out for your meals. You're fed through the hatch, so you never even get out, even for food. (Carol, aged 37)

> Another thing that does disturb me – and I told the officers as well – is that when they say, 'Take the food back to your rooms', there is not a table and chair in the room, you have to eat on your bed. It's unhygenic – and I'm pregnant. (Ruth, aged 18)

> When three of them have to have their food in the cell, it is often stinking. Well, you know how it is if your fridge smells of cauliflower or something. There are dining rooms, so why can't they have their meals in the dining rooms? I think it's because of the bloody laziness of the officers. It's a wonder there's not been a salmonella outbreak – especially when they're not allowed to use bleach in the lavatories. (BOV 1)

> You get access to water but it is limited. The kitchen with drinking water is only open at meal times – three times a day. A lot of people drink the water out of the tap in their rooms and it isn't drinking water at all. They don't have drinking water running through to the dorms, it's only in the kitchens. That itself is ridiculous... Yes, I drink the water in the room. You haven't got a choice. (Liz, aged 19)

Complaints that prisoners do not have the same easy access to doctors that they do outside have been made for years, and, as the end of the century approaches, they continue:

> If you want to see a doctor it's a rigmarole. You have to book and fill in a form saying why. And they have to think you have good reason. It usually takes one or two days to see one. (Deborah, aged 31)

Then, when women do see the doctor they are not convinced that they are being taken as seriously as they would be outside prison. A repeated complaint was that the doctor did not seem to listen to them:

> I remember going through reception and the doctor asked me if I was on any form of drugs and I said I was coming off crack cocaine, and he goes, 'Alright, fine. We'll put you on some medication.' I said, 'Excuse me, I don't want any drugs', and he said, 'It's alright, you'll go on a hospital wing'. And I thought, 'No way'. And I refused completely. I'm a perfectly normal, sane person, and he was ready to put me on a wing where they're just drugged-up through the whole of their sentences. Of course, there's drugs everywhere in prison, and if I had been a very weak person, I could have ended up a heroin addict because there is a lot of heroin inside. (Deborah, aged 31)

> I was very angry, and had refused to be strip-searched, so they put me down the block. When the doctor came to see me, he said that I was obviously very depressed and he could give me some sleeping pills; I was tired, he said. I have never taken sleeping pills, and I was not tired; I was *angry*. When I refused the pills, he just washed his hands off me. (Lindis Percy)

But as well as individual complaints about the medical services, there were also pervasive criticisms of the generally inadequate provision of bathing and washing facilities in the women's prisons, and again the argument was that, because of their different bodily needs and upbringings women prisoners suffer more than men in the area of personal hygiene and personal presentation.

> If you were at home you would have a towel to wipe your bum on and another to wipe your face on; but they have one to last all week. They [prison management] don't take into

account periods and things like that. (Prison Officer 11 – female)

Although women are allowed to wear their own clothes, and although the routines are trying to retain female autonomy, they do still feel that they lose more than men. Whether it's because they're limited as to what food they can buy in the canteen, what face creams and hair shampoos they can buy, it seems to be more important to women using the right shampoo, using the right soap, than it does to a man. (Governor No 6)

Yet, this governor's percipience notwithstanding, it was in the understanding of these specifically female issues of personal cleanliness and self-presentation that male prison staff had been found to be conspicuously lacking. I myself was in a discussion with four long-term prisoners who mentioned that they could not have as many baths as they needed. The male Deputy Governor, who was also present, contradicted them, saying:

That's not true. You can have as many showers as you like.

In reply, all four prisoners spoke at once in their eagerness to make the point: 'Yes, Mr..., but showers are not the same. Women sometimes need a bath, not a shower'. Sadly, as one discussant was later to remark, 'the Dep didn't get it, did he?'. And she sarcastically mimicked his insistence that, 'a shower gets you *clean*, even though you might *prefer* a bath'. At a different prison a similar tale was recounted, this time by a female officer:

Until men have the bodily functions of women, they won't understand it. I mean, the main thing the male governors thought of when we said we needed baths was that we were saying that the women just wanted to soak in a bath, not that they want to get to all the areas and places to be cleansed – you know, give them a good soaking and washing. I mean they're giving no methadone to these women that come in withdrawing from drugs, so they need to soak in a hot bath to ease the aches and cramps. They can't do that stood in a shower. Half of them can't stand up long enough. (Prison Officer, 11 – female)

Additionally, at some gaols, prisoners complained that even when the bathing provision was adequate in itself, the organization of the prison day meant that they had to choose between queuing to make a phone call home and having the bath that they were used to having daily outside prison:

> I didn't have any baths and showers because the only time you could have them was during the half hour when you could use the phone. By the time everyone's got there, there was no way, because the girls that were nearest went into the shower. That was how it was run. You wasn't allowed out for a bath. When I had visits they wouldn't even let me out to wash my hair. (Karen, aged 21)

At other prisons, where women were in shared dormitories, they felt that the washing facilities were inadequate:

> You get a little basin in your room. Now, there's no way you're going to be able to have a shower during the day, because the only time you've got enough time to go to the shower is in the evening, which a lot of people find distressing because they're used to being able to get up in the morning and go and have a shower. I mean, I'm in a dorm here, it's shared between four people, there's one sink and one toilet and you have to take it in turns. (Ruth, aged 18)

The late 1980s and early 1990s saw an acceleration of the programme set up to end the degradation of 'slopping out', by ensuring that all prisoners had access to flush toilets, either through provison of a WC in their cells or by central electronic systems allowing them time-limited access to lavatories outside their cells. Nevertheless, in 1997 women were still being held in cells where no access to flush toilets was being allowed at certain points during the day.

> It's disgusting. There is no sanitation as such in your cell. You're given a potty in your cell when you're locked up between twelve and two and four and five. On a night you're locked up from eight till quarter past nine before the sanitation comes on, and you've got to use this potty. A lot of girls were going through the change and bleeding heavily, had to use these potties and there is no facilities to wash your hands at all. (Kay, aged 46)

> I was in a cell with another woman, and there was a pot. I refused to use it. What I did was, after six I wouldn't drink

anything, because there was no way I was going to use that pot. I didn't use it at all, you know. (Claire, aged 37)

In other prisons a flush lavatory was placed behind curtains, though as one prisoner forcefully expostulated, 'You're still living in a bloody toilet, aren't you?'. More mildly, a NACRO worker made a further salient point: 'With the toilet in the room, you don't get much fresh air circulating'.

A male prison officer had told me that 'living in a dorm can be fun', but prisoners who had been in dormitory accommodation told how they had felt demeaned by having to use a toilet while separated by only a curtain from the room's other occupants:

You can't have any privacy, that was one of the things that shocked me. You can't even go to the toilet – it shocked me having a toilet in your cell with four or five other people. There was a little screen, but there was no door, and you had to go to the toilet in front of everybody, and they would make comments, like, 'Oh, that was a big one', or, 'Ooh, that was a long wee', and you have to take it as a joke. But really it's personal and you don't want people commenting on them sort of things. There was no curtain you could pull and have a wash, and if officers looked in and you were washing, they just looked. (Karen, aged 21)

Older women, in particular, mentioned the lack of privacy for washing themselves as causing especial embarrassment:

While I was in the dormitory, I couldn't wash like those girls do. You know, they just strip off and just wash in front of you. Our generation, we don't do that. I had to wait until I could get to the bathroom, in the afternoon, which I found terrible, as I'm used to a wash first thing every morning. (Rosalie, aged 57)

Not all cells in women's prisons even have a curtain round the lavatory bowl. Women in these cells block up the spyhole in the door, but nonetheless, prisoners have told me that they find the arrangement totally frightening and demeaning, first because of fear of the unsolicited sexual gaze of officers (male or female); and secondly because of the symbolic humiliation of 'living in a lavatory', in a society where sanitary arrangements are usually segregated from domestic quarters.

The main purpose of this chapter has been to discuss the conceptions of approved femininities that inform (and sometimes shape) women's biographies in general and their experiences of imprisonment in particular. It has been demonstrated that both prisoners and staff in the women's institutions are concerned that organizational and disciplinary practices which at first sight appear to be gender-neutral have a different and more pain-inducing impact on women's experience of imprisonment than on men's. In particular, women carry with them into prison all the material consciousness of their family responsibilities; as well as all the ideological baggage about appropriate and legitimated femininities and women's proper place. One consequence is that females in prison are especially vulnerable to the pains of separation from their children; as well as to constant fears about risks to gendered sensibilities whose violation can, in turn, threaten the physical, emotional and sexual composure constitutive of female self-esteem. Women's imprisonment has always been shaped by these social and ideological conditions. In the 1990s, however, the pains of separation from children, together with the fears of actual and symbolic pollution, have been sharpened and amplified: by the organizational consequences of a more punitive sentencing of female offenders (leading to increased prison overcrowding); by tight financial restrictions (resulting in either loss, or continuing lack, of amenity); by the opening up of a prisons front in the 'war on drugs'; by cross gender postings (occasioning complaints about the impropriety of men working in the women's living quarters); and the security fetishism provoked both by a series of escapes from the men's prisons and a Home Secretary determined to show that 'prison works'. The effects on women's imprisonment of this multiple tightening and twisting of the already-gendered penal screw will be examined in Chapter 3.

3 The 1990s – Penal Hammer or Bureaucratic Screw?

The last couple of decades have seen several innovations in the women's prisons. On paper they look good. I am thinking in particular of the many educational initiatives, the personal officer scheme, the introduction of sentence planning, and the opening up of the prisons – to outside groups and prisoner work-schemes and home leaves. Unfortunately, many of those initiatives are now either defunct or exist only in name, on paper.

The reasons for the demise of much that was ameliorative in the women's prisons are complex and difficult to disentangle. In this chapter they will be traced out under six headings: overcrowding; the new fetishism of security; the war on drugs; penal hammer or bureaucratic screw? budgetary and staff cuts; and women prisoners and the politics of difference.

OVERCROWDING

Our job would actually be made much easier if magistrates and High Court judges could actually do their job a bit better, and stop sending us so many people, overcrowding us, and costing the country God knows what for no reason. (Prison Officer 21 – male)

As far as planning goes, there's not even a pretence of it – it's wherever there is a bed. If there's a place at Styal, she'll go to Styal, even if she is from Canterbury. It's a reaction to the space problem that you've got the small add-on prisons, like Winchester and High Point. (Probation Officer 4 – female)

The rapid increase in the female prison population has resulted in an organizational chaos of housing and allocation in the women's prisons which the staff I interviewed referred to as

'the problem of overcrowding' – even in places w
lation of their establishment did not exceed
Normal Accommodation figure on the day of my vis
what they (and prisoners too) were primarily co
about was the way in which the steep rise in the overa
population had occasioned inappropriately hasty alloca,   j,
and transfers between, prisons – with all the attendan mis-
matches of prisoner with institution and prisoner with prisoner,
as well as the anxieties of relatives unable at first to trace, and
then to travel to, their imprisoned loved ones.

> The number of places hasn't kept pace with the number and
> type of women coming in. For example, the women we have
> here [at the Remand Centre] often do not fit the criteria to
> go to an open prison. So we have Drake Hall Prison for open
> condition inmates and no women to send there. We have
> Styal which is dormitory accommodation and the women we
> have do not meet the criteria to go into dormitory accommo-
> dation. So they will be moved down South to Birmingham or
> London, and then they will not be able to maintain the family
> contact. (Prison Officer 11 – female)

> Women's prisons are very busy places, they're horrible places.
> Everybody is running around. They always say they're too
> busy and they *are* very busy. When a woman comes in she sees
> one officer and then she sees another officer, then another
> one, then another one, and they all ask different questions
> and they all insist that they have to separate these functions.
> If you come in and say, 'My child needs to be picked up at
> three o'clock and I'm absolutley terrified there's nobody
> there to do it', it's 'There, there, dear, tell it to...' And it will
> go on and on, and you'll stop telling your story, or be hysteri-
> cal or desperate. If only one person dealt with each inmate it
> would be a much kinder process.
>
> The problem these days is that a lot of the applications we
> can't do anything about because the place is so bloody
> crowded. Everywhere's crowded. It's just hit and miss. For
> instance: somebody has been trained to be a Listener and
> they're suddenly moved – all that training! We had five
> trained Listeners and two were moved out two weeks ago,
> without anyone even contacting the Samaritans. In another
> case: two Ghanaian women, one doesn't speak any English.

And then the one who has no English language is suddenly transferred out without anyone realizing that she doesn't speak a word of English and is absolutely terrified. On the worst days, we will have, say, eight women waiting to go up North. It's getting later and later and later, the prison up North is full and they haven't given the OK. The women haven't told their families, they have a visiting order to come to this prison on Saturday, and they are not allowed to phone because they are only allowed to phone once they get to their new prison. The whole thing is a nightmare, terrible... (BOV 1)

The amount of women in prison is causing horrendous problems in terms of them being transferred, willy nilly, everywhere – up and down the country – at a moment's notice. Example: a woman with two children had them all lined up to come and see her – best bib and tucker and all that – on a Friday afternoon visit. They'd lost a close relative just a few months before and one of the children had taken it very badly. So the relationship with the mother was all-important. She was transferred out of Holloway that Friday morning! (Chris Tchaikovsky, Women in Prison)

A more obvious effect of overcrowding, one that both staff and prisoners were concerned about, was the system's inability to cater effectively for those inmates known to pose special problems of need, danger and risk.

The numbers are particularly high just now [July 1997] and we've been given extra mattresses by the stores office and told that we must double-up on the first landing and put mattresses on the floor. My concern with that is that the majority of women we get in custody are withdrawing very badly off drugs when they come in. So the scenario you end up with is two women in a small room with a toilet and one woman being sick and having terrible diarrhoea – and period problems which is also part of withdrawing – and all in a very small confined space. (Prison Officer 11 – female)

Staff in open prisons were especially critical of the system overload which, they claimed, resulted in their establishments having to take prisoners whose behaviour would not previously have qualified them for open conditions. Concomitantly, they claimed that as a result of these inappropriate allocations they had had to tighten up their regimes to cater for a different type of prisoner. Not unexpectedly, prisoners in the open gaols either claimed that they were finding the regimes more restrictive than those of the closed prisons, or that because of the combination of open conditions and stricter regimes, they felt more at risk of getting into trouble and (possibly) facing disciplinary charges. For some governors of open prisons the problem was that better conditions in the closed prisons made the open conditions less attractive, and therefore, again, they had to tighten physical security when the dynamic controls emanating from the incentives to remain in a superior environment no longer obtained:

> Because it used to be so horrific in the closed prisons, the conditions here were marvellous compared with Durham or Holloway, and they actually were grateful: 'Yes, Ma'am, thank you Ma'am, I won't put a foot wrong, Ma'am' etc. Now the pressures are such that (a) we haven't got the vacancies in the closed prisons to turn them back to, so we've got to manage them. And secondly, the conditions in closed prisons are so much better than they were that they can say, 'Well, I got my own room there, I've got to live in a dormitory here' and there's no incentive for them to want to stay here. Especially, like, for the Londoners or anyone else that will lose their visits because it's too far for people to come to. (Governor, No 4)

In all institutions staff talked about the difficulties of monitoring prisoners (and especially those vulnerable to bullying or at risk of self-harm), when the whole of the women's system is so physically overloaded and understaffed (see below).

> For instance, property goes missing more when they are being moved around so much, as they are at the moment, as a result of the overcrowding. Where there's a bed, there's a body and they just keep shuffling people round. You can't get to know your prisoners so well. (Governor No 2 – female)

Interestingly, research on male prisoners in the United States has found that the inmates most likely to suffer from high blood pressure were first-time offenders and those placed in dormitory accommodation (Ostfeld *et al.* 1987:179, 190), a finding very relevant to Britain's first-time women offenders, many of whom find dormitory living either threatening or painful.

Staff in two establishments mentioned the sexual assaults that had occurred when young prisoners known to be 'at risk' had been made more vulnerable by overcrowding and the resulting diminution of close staff surveillance.

> We had such trouble here with women giving each other internals that with the shortage of staff we actually refused to unlock one evening, and it was subject to an inquiry. And there were literally chaplains, nurses and prisoners wanting to go on the investigation to tell them about the internal [vaginal] searching [by prisoners looking for hidden drugs] that was going on. I mean there were women going to the nurses with bruises between their legs where they had been forcibly held down, and too frightened to take it to the police. (Prison Officer 11 – female)

When prisoners themselves complained to me about overcrowding, they did not mention fear of sexual assault by other prisoners as being foremost among their many worries, (though this may have been because those most in fear of 'decrutching' were those whom other inmates may have had good reasons for suspecting of hiding contraband drugs on their persons, and who would therefore be very circumspect about drawing anyone's attention to their predicament). But many prisoners were eloquent about their fears of being locked up with violent or mentally ill inmates

> Of course you get fighting. If someone gets drugs in and doesn't tell anyone else, then they beat them up and take it off them – decrutch they call it. C1 is for psychiatric people and they get banged up for twenty four hours a day. I know one girl down there who's always behind her door, because when she comes out she attacks the officers. But she can't help it. She should be in a hospital, not in a prison. It's not the place for her. If they do start up they just put them in a strip cell, just keep feeding them drugs. Most of them are doped up most of the time. It's terrible. (Annie, aged 28)

> There are a lot of mentally ill women that should be in the block that aren't in the block. Women that are schizophrenic in prison are allowed on a normal block. That's not right, it's dangerous, and you never know when you are going into a cell with a mad person – someone who's murdered and got no

remorse, doesn't give a shit and would do it again. (Karen, aged 21)

And if that strikes you as being a bit melodramatic, listen now to Lyn (who actually was incarcerated while she was experiencing a mental breakdown) and Vera (just one of several prisoners for whom the fear of attack became the reality):

I was going round all over Christmas 1995, very, very depressed. I'd lit a few fires before that, just trying to harm myself. I was really, really depressed, totally and absolutely and utterly depressed. I couldn't even get out of the house, I didn't want to eat. The neighbours were out and I was really, really rock bottom. I just went and burnt this carpet, and then I burnt some papers, and they fell to the floor. It wasn't anybody else I wanted to harm, it was myself, just myself... I was taken by this police officer under the Mental Health Act and eventually I was charged with arson and intent to endanger lives. So that was what led up to it. [While on remand, Lyn was at Risley and was in no trouble. After being sentenced to two years imprisonment, she was sent to Eastwood Park Prison.] I was taken to my cell which was more like a cage than a cell – very, very small with barely enough room to move round... I felt very nervy and very scared, very apprehensive about what was happening, very claustrophobic. Because I tried to set fire to the nightdress I was wearing, I was moved down to the hospital wing. You could say that was where the real nightmare started. I set fire to all my clothes, so all the furniture was taken out of my room and I was made to sleep on the floor in just a strip dress with no underwear or anything. It was totally degrading and I was freezing cold and totally depressed. It seemed that no-one cared what happened to me. I felt so humiliated at these awful conditions that I found myself in, I smashed a loo seat, and I was segregated. I then went into a kind of fit and I barricaded the door by putting my bed behind it. It was frustration at being treated like an animal. Next they moved me down to the block. Apparently I'd gone for one of the staff and I didn't even know I'd done it. It's not their fault, they're not trained as psychiatric nurses. I was so angry and upset I stuck a knife inside me. They got it out, but I felt locked away and not a human body. I remember throwing soup up the wall and I remember I was in a wet strip dress. Then I was naked. I asked a nurse, 'How long am I going to stay in this room?' And I was naked and freezing cold. She just stood outside, staring at me through the glass. I said, 'How long am I going to stay here?' She said, 'As long as it takes'. Next day they sent me to Holloway, and I settled down there. (Lyn, aged 37)

She'd come out of a mental hospital. The prison had put her on the wrong location – she should have been on the psychiatric wing, C1. I was fast asleep in bed and she cut my face. She said it was because I had nice cheekbones! (Laughs) There was so much blood, it was terrible. She rung the buzzer and five officers came running, and she gave the razor up. They said, 'So you admit doing Vera's face?' and she said 'yes' straight away and that there was no reason for it. I had eleven butterfly stitches and sixteen normal stitches. She's got to go to court for that, but the scar will never go away. I just try to keep my hair over it. (Vera, aged 28)

THE NEW FETISHISM OF PRISON SECURITY

The Review of Prison Security (Home Office 1995b) which was presented to Home Secretary Michael Howard by General Sir John Learmont in October 1995 made recommendations which did not fall on stony ground. Michael Howard had already insisted publicly and repeatedly that 'prison works', and appeared more than willing to do whatever might be thought necessary to restore the Prison Service's credibility after the escapes first from Whitemoor Prison and then from Parkhurst. Indeed, his own punitive reforms (such as cutting back on home leave) were mainly implemented with a view to appeasing a tabloid press critical of a system seen to be both soft on offenders, and worse, incapable of keeping violent prisoners in custody. Thus, although the Woodcock and Learmont Inquiries had been set up in response to escapes from men's prisons, and although, too, the Learmont Report itself recognized that the characteristics of the female prison population are very different to those of the male prison population, all the new security measures, whatever their authorship, were implemented right across the system – regardless of gender. Among the changes which both staff and female prisoners considered most inappropriate to women's gaols were those involving the curtailment of temporary release and home leave; and the handcuffing of prisoners under escort. (There were others, primarily relating to strip searches and urine tests, but these will be discussed below in the section on the 'war on drugs'.)

The Director General's Tale

By 1995 we faced an enormous programme of new initiatives – security changes following Whitemoor and Parkhurst, severe curtailment of home leave with entirely new criteria being applied, a major crackdown on drugs with the introduction of drug testing, and a wholesale restructuring of privileges for prisoners based on the principle of earning through good behaviour. None of these changes was popular with prisoners. In one way or another they would all make life in prison more irksome and more unpleasant. (Derek Lewis, Director General of The Prison Service, 1992–95 in Lewis 1997:223–24)

BOV Member's Comment

It's what we're fighting the whole time, this insistence upon physical, visible, oppressive security. Then, the idea that, having so structured and straight-jacketed people, you can turn them out into the world outside, where's there's no structure, probably no job, nothing, nothing to get up for in the morning... and that somehow they're going to carry on in that way. I just can't see it working. (BOV 3 – female)

The Governors' Tales

We were moving along very nicely until Whitemoor. Then Whitemoor hit and the Woodcock Report came out and from then on all the security measures were implemented across the board – from the handcuffing of prisoners on escort to the same criteria for home leave or temporary release, to drug testing. Between Woodcock and Learmont all those things have been overlaid on to the female system. But it's a very small percentage of female prisoners who need the same levels of security that we're talking about in the male system.

All discretion has gone. One of the saddest things I heard was a woman saying: 'I am not going to the child custody hearing because if I have to go in handcuffs with two prison officers, the picture that I will present is not a picture I want to give to my children or to the panel'.

Why are we talking about all this security when for years I would grant temporary release to a female prisoner, just in recognition of the female role in the family unit? For instance, for child custody hearings I would send a prison officer but the prisoner would be licensed. The prison officer would only be there as emotional support, not to make sure the prisoner didn't escape but to make sure that if the custody hearing was gruelling or went wrong, there was someone there to pick up on the woman afterwards. Because she was going to feel pretty bad about it. Dying relatives, funerals... and I have on occasion given a woman temporary release to take her child to school on its first day at school, because that's a milestone in a child's life. If we're talking about getting these women out of the trap of under-achieving and their children out of under-achieving, then school's a very big issue. And I have to say that the number of times I have been let down by a woman is negligible. Even if they don't return, we know where they are; they're not going to be marauding around Woolworths with bloody machetes or shotguns.

I know of a woman in one prison who has a lump in her breast, but she will not go to hospital because she knows she would have to go in handcuffs – she's not yet reached the criteria to be granted temporary release according to the gospel according to Michael Howard. (Governor No 2 – female)

Women don't need the same kind of physical security levels that their male counterparts do. By and large, too, female prisoners do not rise to the vulnerable prisoners [ie prisoners convicted of crimes that other inmates find especially abhorrent.] Our vulnerable prisoners can walk through the establishment with an officer without any kind of fear of any kind of attack – either verbal or physical – from the other inmates.

A lot of the handcuffing issues – it's got to be said – came about because of the scares about escorting male prisoners.

Certainly with visists to dying relatives they have to remain handcuffed unless we specify that the handcuffs can be removed. What is called for nowadays is to give fairly precise directions to the staff who are doing escorts. It actually removes discretion. (Governor No 1 – male)

One of the problems at the moment is this obsession with security and building fences around people. The reality is that all these policies are geared for men, it's actually men who failed the system, who've fouled-up over temporary release, that have caused the cutbacks there. There's very few women who will scale the prison walls. OK, I think there were three at Holloway, but the usual fact of the matter is that *men run from prison* whereas *women will run to home*. It's usually because of bad news from home they will abscond. OK, there are a percentage of women who are violent, who need locking up, but they are very few compared with men.

We regret that temporary release has been curtailed. Nobody disagrees with risk assessments but we are restricted with women because whereas men go to the gymnasium and pump iron, or go to the football field and kick a ball about, if you try to organize PE for women, they don't want to know. But if you say, 'It's a nice day, how about a bike ride?' Or, 'Let's go for a walk or hike or something', they'll do it. Now, of course, with the temporary release restrictions, it's very difficult to do those sort of things. Hopefully, because of a lot of shouting by myself and others, Headquarters are now rediscovering that there are differences and that women's needs are different. Nobody is saying that if the woman committed the crime she needn't do the time; but it's a matter of how it's managed. (Governor No 4 – male)

The Prison Officers' Tales

We've got the heightened security now and it's affecting everything – visits, days out shopping, funerals, hospital appointments, everything. We used to be able to use our discretion, but now it's all according to the security manual, 'You will be cuffed'. You're not allowed to like your work any more. I mean, we never used to cuff them. Increased security's also stopped things like days out for lifers. That is a big bone of contention for me, because it was something they could aim for, you could use it not as a stick, but as a sort of carrot. (Prison Officer 1 – female)

Security changes are changing the regimes because they are tightening things up. Like at one time the Chaplain used to run a Chaplaincy Group in the evening, but now the security department has said the Chapel is not secure, because it's only a prefabricated building. So they can't go to that in the evening, that takes away that group. It's only a small thing but it's a change. It's not hard to jack- up security, anybody can do that, but the trick, of course, is to get the balance between activities, regimes and security. Now might be the time to say we've got too much security. Certainly, in my experience there is no control problem here, the changes are all to do with the internal politics of the prison system. I don't personally know of a female gaol that has ever suffered mass disturbance in recent times. (Prison Officer 3 – male)

We knew there was going to be a major tightening up of the temporary release system, but we didn't know that it was going to have such a dramatic effect so quickly. Things like that are usually phased in. But this! One day it wasn't there and the next day it was – and everybody had to comply with it. Certainly the effect on some of the lifers was devastating. They were asking the same type of questions as us: 'How come yesterday I could walk down to the village, to start to reintegrate myself, and today you're telling me that I need an escort and possibly handcuffs?' If a woman's been in a long time, we need to be getting her out, look for accommodation, give her a chance to go out there and see what it's like. The situation now is ridiculous and crazy. (Prison Officer 7 – female)

The Prisoners' Tales

I had bronchitis one time and they took me to the hospital for an x-ray. That was horrible, because you've got two prison officers with you and you have to sit in a waiting room handcuffed – which isn't very nice you know. (Carol, first offender aged 37, serving 12 months for supplying a Class A drug)

I was handcuffed to a bed for three weeks for the abscess in my lung. Governor's orders they said. Now, I had a drip in my arm and I had a chest drain up my back – I don't know where they thought I was going to in that state! Every time I wanted to go to the toilet I was on them dog chains – feel like an animal on them. I'm sick, I'm very ill, I'm not feeling very well, and I'm handcuffed to a bed. Everytime I wanted to go to the toilet they used to say, 'Walkies?' I kept trying to hide the handcuffs, but he [the officer] wouldn't have it. Especially when I went into the x-ray room there was no way I could go anywhere out of the windows, but they still wouldn't un-hand-cuff. Now the doctor made them take the handcuffs off me for an x-ray, because you can't x-ray people with metal on. (Liz, aged 19 convicted of robbery)

The Governor said I had to go handcuffed to the funeral. So I went to see the PO and told him I wasn't going because of the handcuffs, because my niece and nephew actually work for the police and it would have been embarrassing for them. He said that I might be sorry afterwards if I didn't go, and told me to think about it. So I went and phoned my family and they said they wanted me there, even in handcuffs. So we went by car and there was an officer either side of me and I was handcuffed. I didn't really want to go under them cir-cumstances, but they tried to cover up the handcuffs as best they could. (Kay, aged 46, first offender, not a drug user, serving 12 months for a drugs-related offence)

Now, in 1997, it has become routine for official prison public-ations to lament the lack of knowledge that there is about female prisoners. But, as will be apparent from the above, there is, (and has been for several hundred years), an immense amount of knowledge about the harrowing social circumstances of many women prisoners, and a great deal of expertise, humanity and concern in relation to their special needs when in prison. The problem, therefore, has not been that the knowl-edge has not been there, but that its main custodians have been low-paid women workers (ie female prison officers), a group notoriously absent from the corridors of power. As a result, their expert knowledge on female prisoners has seldom (if ever) been recognized as such, nor, on the rare occasions when it has been, has there been the political will to use it. Likewise, and as

I shall argue at greater length in Chapter 4, over the years the Prison Service has had available to it many examples of good practice from around the world. But the arrogance of office exhibited in the past by some officials at Prison Service Headquarters has led them to exhibit a level of complacency about English prisons which I, for one, have found breathtaking (even though it has been documented by others (eg Cohen and Taylor 1978; Lewis 1997). For instance, when I asked a Governor Grade 4 working at Headquarters in 1997, if the Prison Department ever followed the example of other countries, and particularly in relation to running the women's system, she replied:

> We are aware of what goes on elsewhere, but it's usually a matter of them learning from us.

Which reminded me of the prison governor who, in the 1980s, told me:

> We visit places abroad, and we keep up with developments in other countries. But we seldom see anything which would work here. We have our own traditions.

It is this complacency at Prison Service Headquarters, together with the way in which politicians and the media have between them used the prisons as a political football (which every one can carelessly kick around with impunity), that has caused resentment amongst prison staff at all levels and in all departments. (Especially when, according to several prison personnel, so many of the prison fiascos of recent times have been own goals scored by the Home Office itself.) Specifically, prison staff have been outraged that, as a result of the security blueprints which have been laid down for them, they have been deprived of the use of so much of their professional discretion – a necessary tool in volatile situations requiring sensitive rule interpretation and innovative management.

> We have to manage life prisoners – it is quite a job, especially when they are waiting for parole decisions. Now we are not supposed to second guess what the Board will do, but we used to feel that we could give women some guidance about how they were doing in the prison, what we thought of them – even if we had to say that we couldn't say what the final

outcome would be. But now we're all at sea on everything. You cannot give an opinion on anything, anything may happen from day to day. And I think that, as a result, the prisoners have less confidence in us. They see the way we're treated, and they know that sometimes we are no more knowledgeable about what's going on in the system than they are. (Prison Officer 2 – female)

Closely related to the security crises of the 1990s and the subsequent inquiries into them is the 'culture of blame' which appears to have added a further dimension to the difficulties under which prison staff labour. And it appears to be a wholly unproductive development.

Previously officers used their discretion more than they do now. Because of the blame culture that's around at the moment, discretion is a word that's not used. If you deviate from the straight and narrow now – and I'm only talking about circumventing some of the pettier little rules – you're more likely to get sacked. This blame culture is making all staff consider their own positions. There are Governors who still take risks, but at tremendous personal risk, tremendous personal risk. (Governor No 2 – female)

Governors appeared to feel this risk pressing most heavily upon them when it came to 'risk-assessing' women applying to be temporarily absent from the prison under the temporary leave, home leave or community visit provisions.

If a prisoner goes out of the gate wrongly, it doesn't matter what any other Governor is doing, because it is down to you. You might have decided on a common policy with other governors, but what matters is that you did the risk assessment. (Governor No 6 – male)

Risk-assessment is an essentially risky business, and because no rule ever fits every situation and contingency, it is accepted that all who make these assessments are themselves at risk of making mistakes:

I'm in the middle of doing risk-assessments now – for all sorts of things – people going to hospital, wanting to go to college interviews, funerals – you name it, we'll risk-assess it! We now even risk-assess people who want to work on the garden party! But, at the end of the day, we're dealing with human beings and they're not totally predictable. So sometimes we get it wrong through no fault of our own. (Governor No 5 – male)

Discretion over how rules are applied is one of the powers that a society usually accords to its professionals – on the understanding that, in situations where difficult judgements have to be made, persons with such a complex of professional knowledge will make the safest decisions. However, during the 1980s and 1990s it has increasingly become the case that public sector professionals and middle managers have had displaced on to them the blame for catastrophies which have been less of their own making and more the fault of their political and administrative masters' failure to develop coherent and consistent policies. Nowhere has this been more apparent than in the Prison Service, where prison governors have again and again had to carry the can for all that has gone wrong in the gaols, while the relevant ministers and civil servants have been at perpetual loggerheads with one another, the clearest 'message' emerging from their often confused and contradictory policy statements being that the only 'right' decisions on sentencing, prison policy, or any other criminal matter are those that will pass the 'Sun test' (ie be approved by the Sun newspaper). This situation, where prison governors and other criminal justice professionals have been saddled with heavier responsibilities while being relieved of most of their discretionary powers, has been further aggravated by the lack of a holistic framework in which the comprehensive risk-assessments which have to be made by a variety of criminal justice players can be accomplished. Thus, for example, different Probation Services have different procedures for the making of risk-assessments – and they are not necessarily easily understood by the staff of the prison where the final decision has to be made. A probation officer gave an example of the ensuing frustration that can be experienced by both staff and prisoners:

I'm working on a case at the moment which seems very hard. The woman is on a three year sentence but she's served a lot of time remanded in custody, so in fact she's within six months of her release now. She's not being allowed out on a community visit – which is within a twenty mile radius of the prison, because we've had no enquiries made of the victim yet. We have not been able to get those back from the probation officer. The prison finds it hard to understand that each probation service has its own way of doing it. There's no national probation service, as you know, and each probation service is at a different stage of creating, formulating, a victims' policy. So some areas are very well up in it and others aren't. This authority that I'm working with does not have a coherent policy as yet and victim enquiries are very low on their list of priorities. Meanwhile, this woman cannot go out on her community visit until the victim enquiries are done. (Probation Officer 2 – male)

But although lack of organization and leadership from above was one major source of grievance amongst the prison staff whom I interviewed, some of their most caustic comments were reserved for the craven and politically expedient way in which governments have recently conflated press opinions with public opinion.

'Running a holiday camp?' 'Be more harsh with them?' The *Sun* says things like that to sell newspapers. I'm not here to punish anybody. My function is to keep them for the court and treat them with humanity. If people want prisoners stacked up five or six to a cell or people beaten up against the wall, well, put it in our contract ... But then the *Sun,* the *same Sun newspaper, mind,* will turn around and be calling me a barbarian – to sell newspapers. That's what the newspaper business is about. Meanwhile, I'm quite proud of what I'm doing. I've got to plough on – and I suppose that somewhere along the line someone will give a lead. (Prison Officer 13 – male)

Getting rid of TVs in prisoners' cells! That was another proposal that showed that Howard didn't know what he was talking about. Mind you, he most likely suggested it with the *Sun* newspaper in mind. In this prison we have the press on to us every day asking about certain prisoners. Our instructions are to make no comment. So then they make it up, repeat it to us over the phone; we say, 'No comment', and then they print what *they* said as if by not denying it you are confirming it. (Governor No 8 – male)

A young lifer was sent out to Leeds on a shopping expedition, on a shopping trip. This was picked up by the press and caused a right old hoohah, so much so that the Department issued a press notice condemning the Governor of that prison for what he'd done. Now in my view that press notice was too harsh, and shouldn't have been done. Anyhow, as a result of that one incident, lifers were then not allowed to go out shopping or hiking or swimming at all. (Governor No 1 – male)

I know that the government has to recognize public opinion. But the public seem to be fed things from the newspapers and then not question what they read. Then the government *reacts* to public opinion, but it doesn't really *respond* to public opinion. (BOV 3 – female)

THE WAR AGAINST DRUGS

Everything we do has to pass the 'drugs test'. The whole logic and organization of this prison is now directed at waging war on drugs. Personally, I don't think that should be the main aim of a prison. (Governor of a women's prison in New Zealand, 1996)

The obsession about drugs in prison is whipped up as ever by the *Sun* newspaper and its tabloid brothers and sisters. How do they assume we are going to keep drugs out of prisons when drugs are a way of life outside prison? All prison ever does is reflect a small microcosm of what's going on outside of prison! This whole idea that drugs are the sole domain of the criminal fraternity is absolute bullshit – because the designer drugs are very much a middle-class issue. (Governor No 2 – female)

Until you can just dig a hole in the ground and put a prisoner in it and throw the food in every day, you'll never stop drug trafficking. All prisons can do is to respond by education – about what drugs can do to you; and then supporting them while they are coming off. But some don't want to come off, and some who take cannabis don't accept that it should be illegal. So it's not even a simple issue of right and wrong like other crimes. (Governor No 4 – male)

Although the only drugs officially allowed to prisoners are
those which have been medically prescribed for specific prisoners, illicit drugs (including alcohol) have always been obtain-
able in prisons. However, since the mid 1990s, concern with the
illicit possession and use of drugs by prisoners has increased
and, as was outlined in Chapter 1, many more security measures to detect hidden drugs have been introduced. Chief among
them have been the use of dogs to reveal the presence of illicit
drugs; the searching of staff; the searching of all visitors,
including children and babies; the mandatory drugs testing of
prisoners through urine samples taken both randomly and 'on
suspicion'; and the formation of dedicated search teams trained
specially to search rooms, property and inmates.

Governors to whom I spoke had mixed views about the use-
fulness of these innovations in general and especially about
their appropriateness to the women's prisons. The main arguments for and against the acceleration of the fight to keep
drugs out of the prisons have already been outlined in Chapter
1 (see p. 34). The measures taken against drugs are discussed
again now in this chapter because they have been among some
of the more contentious of the security measures introduced
into women's prisons in the wake of the Woodcock and
Learmont Inquiries into security in men's prisons. They have
certainly not made relationships between staff and inmates any
easier and many staff, as well as inmates, have claimed that
they have caused much more penal pain in the women's institutions than in the men's.

The BOV's Tale

The whole drugs thing is a complete and utter disaster.
Physical security for women is so repressive and it runs counter
to everything we're trying to do. You're trying to buid them up,
you're trying to give them a sense of identity, you're trying to
build their self-esteem, and then you've got them peeing into a
pot for mandatory drug testing in front of an officer. I could
weep for some of them, particularly the older women. I think I
would just up-end the table, I couldn't take it.

The officers here are very good, they don't like having to do
the job, but I do just wonder why we're doing it, random
testing, at public expense, people who have never had any

involvement with drugs and there's no suspicion of drugs, no history of drugs. I'm all for cracking the drug problem, but I do think that targeting it might be a more sensible thing to do. (BOV 3 – female)

The Governors' Tales

The drug testing is causing prisoners tremendous distress at the moment, trmendous distress. It's a Michael Howard design, along with many others. He makes the blanket decisions and doesn't take account of the special difficulties that women face. He's done this throughout his time as Home Secretary, despite representations, I have to say, from very many people, including the Prison Governors' Association, NACRO, Prison Reform Trust, Penal Affairs Consortium and all those sort of people.

Of course we don't allow them to have drugs in prisons, and where we find them we stop it. But to actually batten down the hatches is just appallingly stupid. We've become obsessed with it. And if, as is claimed, women are changing from soft drugs to harder drugs because of the shorter period of time they stay in the urine, then it's a very irresponsible thing for us to be doing. Because I know many people who have happily smoked dope since the 1960s because it's the thing we all did then. I, too, smoked marijuana, and many people have never progressed beyond that. I suspect that it is used by some prison staff at weekends, in a club somewhere. So prison staff can't get too steamed up about it, about cannabis. Governors wouldn't encourage it, wouldn't dream of encouraging it, but this obsession with trying to stop it has a damaging effect.

For instance, women will say they don't want their children to visit because they don't want them searched, and I can understand that. One woman said to me, 'Look, I don't want my children to grow up with an anti-authority attitude, and if a uniformed person starts searching my children when they come to visit me, what is it saying to my children? 'These people invade your privacy.' Now this woman has never taken drugs in her life, it's not why she's in prison, so why should her children be subjected to it? It's too distressing for her so she's not seeing her children. That to me is so damaging. And then the knock-on effects on that family, the damage to that family unit in the long-term ... it just bears no scrutiny.

But that's the environment we're working in at the moment, and I'm sure some of my colleagues would agree with me. But I have to say that I can't name them. The majority of my colleagues whom I converse with on a regular basis cannot see the point, but it's a matter of obeying the last instruction because if you don't you're culpable, and if you are culpable you are going to be blamed. The Inspectorate is in favour of the old, post-Woolf model of running the women's prisons, but while the numbers continue to go up, and there is no relaxation in this rigidity about lack of discretion – all criteria must be met as laid down – there's little hope of any governor being able to run that [more humane] kind of prison. (Governor No 2 – female)

The sample testing of 10 per cent per month is done by computer, and personally a lot of us think it is a farce. Because we got better results by targeting people who, we knew, were taking it. The majority of the ones we do now come back negative. The prisoners are absolutely aware that cannabis stays in the bloodstream for a lot longer than hard drugs, so there are some anecdotal stories of people switching from cannabis to hard drugs, because there is less risk of being caught. There is very little evidence of hard drugs here or of needles. Mandatory drug testing is a disincentive to waverers who might be tempted to use it but I don't think it ever puts off those who are determined. In cost effective terms it just isn't. It isn't cost effective because we test an awful lot of people who would never touch it. It's also the indignity of all that. We're saying, 'We're treating you with respect – now, come and pee in a bucket'. It's not on. (Governor No 4 – male)

We've been doing it for something like fifteen months now, and only two or three prisoners have refused. I mean, the prisoners don't like it, because it is a pretty degrading activity, however you do it. Interestingly, though, whenever we try to do something to reduce drugs in the prison, there is quite a large element of the prisoners who welcome that. (Governor No 5 – male)

And the accuracy of this last comment was borne out by much
of what the prisoners had to say to me about drugs. MDT was
just one more prison indignity that had to be endured, though
several said that they appreciated the need to control drugs in
an environment where possession of them could provoke fights
and sexual assault. Where they were critical of MDT was when
it was carried out on people never known to have taken drugs or
when it was conducted in a manner causing unnecessary loss of
dignity. Indeed, some prisoners expressed a suspicion that, far
from being random drug testing, the officers chose women
whom they knew had never taken drugs in order to keep down
the numbers of prisoners testing positive in their establishments. As one prisoner put it:

> It seems odd that they keep on picking on someone who has
> never taken drugs, when all of us can see the ones who're
> on something. And if we can see it, the officers can. (Annie,
> aged 28)

(For further evidence on the indignities associated with MDT,
see Dockley 1996; Her Majesty's Chief Inspector of Prisons
1997a; 1997b.) What prisoners complained about even more
than the drug testing, however, was the excessive number of
strip searches which they were being given in the name of the
stepped-up security.

The Prisoners' Tales

> I was picked by a computer and obviously I knew I was going
> to be negative – if it was positive I would want to know the
> reason why. I think it's a good idea, but it's not going to stop
> the drugs.
>   Two women officers come for you and they take you down
> the block and they take you through where there's no
> windows in the room – it's so tiny. There's a little shelf there,
> and she reads everything to you, and gives you this little con-
> tainer, a plastic-like cup. Then she says, 'You do a urine in
> there', and she tells you to go into the toilets. You close the
> door, but there's a glass panel in the door, and she says, 'I
> have to stand out here and look in'. They make you wash your
> hands first, but there is no soap there. Then you go into the
> toilet and you have to wee into this container. She's there

watching you, in the little window, and then when you come out you hand it to her. She puts it in these two things, seals them down, you sign them, and she goes through all these questions about are you on drugs. And at that time I was on medication because I had trouble with gall stones. I told her that, and she said, 'Don't worry we'll just check it with the hospital' – and it come back negative. (Mya, aged 34)

I wondered what the hell was going on. But one of these DSTs [member of Dedicated Search Team) realized that it must all be strange to me and she come over to me and she did explain what happened when you got into the room. She said, 'We have to do it, it's just part of our job. We're not saying you have drugs, we just have to do it'.

They have to completely search the room, lift the beds up and everything, look in all your cupboards and things. Then each one of you are taken in individually and there are two women in the room these red and blacks [Dedicated Search Team]- and you are strip-searched. You don't take everything off in one go, you know, you take a certain amount off and they check through that. So you've always got something on, but at my age, you know! It was terrible, terrible. If I saw a drug I wouldn't know it was a drug, because I've had no dealing with them. They've searched the room since, but they said it was a token search because they do know me. But they said, 'We just have to do it'. (Rosalie, aged 57)

There are people you can tell are on drugs, but they never seem to get tested. Yet some poor, old, nervous lady gets taken and tested. I think that's a waste of money. (Jan, aged 44)

You could get someone that's never taken a drug in their life, but if they have a visit they'll strip-search them. You all go through it. As soon as you go into another prison you have to get strip searched again, even when you're going with security. (Annie, aged 28)

These MDTs, these drug tests are really daft. The whole thing is ridiculous because you're just getting more smack-heads in prison. I've had a test and it came back negative. I don't think any of us like to be stripped off and told to pee into a little dish for a drug test. It's so degrading when they have to strip you off and they're looking at your body. I mean, that's private, sort of, your body is the sort of thing you should only show your partner, not anyone else. They do it quite properly, but it's still degrading. You lose all dignity, don't you? (Cheryl, aged 20)

[In reception] I had a shower. You put your gown on, and then you have to do a twirl behind the curtain. The indignity of it! Later they did one half at a time – you know, you don't have to take your bra off, just lift it up, and just take your underpants down to your knees. What made it so awful was that you were behind this curtain and anybody could walk through the Reception room. (Claire, aged 37)

I had a urine test and they made you squat. It's bad enough doing it in front of a bloke, but doing it in front of a woman is even worse. They pat you down a hell of a lot and you're thinking that it's a woman who's doing it, and if she's gay, I find that worse than having a bloke. All your privacy is totally invaded, isn't it? They make you squat and they ask you to cough. If you're having a period, you don't want to be doing something like that, do you? But if you refuse, you get three days straight away. (Carol, aged 37)

On every cell search that I've seen they [Dedicated Search Teams] all dressed in black combat gear. They looked a bit like karate people. Once the prison was closed down for three days because some drugs had gone missing, and they searched every single cell, did these people.
They did strip searches, too. They were very humiliating. My main objection was that they were lesbians. It's bad enough being strip-searched, without being strip-searched by lesbians. But when I wrote to the Governor about this, he asked me if I was questioning their sexuality. So it was a little bit of a sore point with them and although those officers were fair officers, I didn't want to be strip-searched and squatted by them. I did feel degraded. They even take your sanitary towel off you. They go between your toes, and say, 'bend over', you know.
The thing I always find unbelievable – I went to a funeral in October and the prison officer come to my cell for me and I was still getting dressed when she came. She took me to Reception. I was strip-searched in Reception. I was handcuffed

to two officers to and from the funeral, and strip-searched
again when I went back into the prison. Now, I'd been handcuffed to two prison officers for the whole of the journey, for
the whole of the funeral. And they strip-searched me going
back in! (Kay, aged 46)

PENAL HAMMER, OR BUREAUCRATIC SCREW?

There is a negative culture in women's prisons, and much of
it is very punitive. This is all part of the Howard syndrome.
The other day, for instance, it was just absolutely ludicrous,
the commandment came down that prisoners must not be
seen to be enjoying themselves, *whatever* it is they are doing.
(Senior Official in Home Office)

One of the main difficulties of discussing women's imprisonment as we approach the millennium, is that in recent years
most of the official documents on prisons in general, and
women's imprisonment in particular, are replete with arguments that the secure prison will be one that is based upon
dynamic, rather than repressive, security; in other words, security that is both cemented by, and the product of, good relationships between staff and prisoners, meaningful activities and an
effective structure of privileges and incentives. Now, leaving
aside the old-fashioned notion that incarceration itself is the
punishment, and that prisoners should not suffer additional
deprivations other than those that are integral to keeping them
in custody, leaving that aside for a moment, it has to be said
that the main problem with dynamic security, as far as the
women's prisons in England are concerned, is that attempts to
put it into practice have been either nullified or swamped by
straightforwardly repressive changes – often instigated by government ministers and the media – that pull in an entirely different direction to the liberal sentiments of the official reports;
or, ironically, they have been subverted by their own accompany-
ing excesses of bureaucracy. Furthermore, even where prison
staff have put in a great deal of time to ensure that new
schemes and systems are in place, financial restrictions have
too often prevented those schemes from ever becoming fully
operative. As a result, much of what has been good in the

official reports of recent years, has functioned much, and merely, as the cynics said it would – to paper over the cracks in an overburdened, confused, and self-defeating system.

As I talked to people in the women's prisons, I asked staff and prisoners about three recent innovations: the Personal Officer and Sentence Planning Schemes, involving the allocation of a personal officer to prisoners serving over 12 months, to be central to planning the sentence (see Chapter 1 p. 33); and the Incentives and Earned Privileges Scheme (see Chapter 1 p. 32). Their replies helped me to understand why so many prisoners talked about the chaos in the women's prisons, and also why prisoners got so worked up as they talked to me about what they saw as the arbitrary and unfair working of the Incentives and Earned Privileges Scheme.

> I think the Personal Officer Scheme can help because the inmate can actually identify with a member of staff. But like everything else, I don't think it's done properly. We're not given any time to do it. I've got one girl, and she'll shout, 'I want to see you', and I haven't got any time to see her. Four officers got sentence planning off the ground, but again, it's one of the things, if there's staff shortages, it's pulled out. But it's a good idea, especially for someone doing a long sentence, cos then if someone says, 'She's nowt but a bloody toe-rag', you can put the other side of the coin. (Prison Officer 1)

> The Personal Officer Scheme and Sentence Planning has made no difference to me. It's very difficult to get them done because they're so busy. I saw the Chaplain, I saw education for two minutes and the doctor – he just said, 'How are you? Alright? Goodbye. See you later'. Then I assumed that my personal officer would come along and chat to me but she did not speak to me once. (Amanda, aged 48)

> Difference they've made? Personal Officer and Sentence Planning? Truthfully? Nothing. Nothing. That is a purely paperwork activity. We do the paper. We do see the women, obviously, and they get told, 'You've got a personal officer'. But the shifts that we're on, we're not always available, and sometimes it can portray the wrong image. They may wait a couple of weeks to see a personal officer, then see somebody else, when it could have been dealt with a lot sooner. It's

purely lip service to the Prison Service, to be honest. Women can be given a pep talk, plus we send off the paperwork to probation, but we never get any feedback. So no, I don't think it does make any difference. Plus the young offenders – we have to do a sentence plan on all young offenders. They may only be serving six weeks. There's nothing whatsoever we can do – so that's a waste of time. We've got so many prisoners coming in all the time. The rapport with prisoners used to be brilliant, but now we don't get to know half of the problems because we're based in the office, and we've got that much paperwork to do that we don't actually get round. There's too much paperwork, it's all paperwork now. I would say about 75 per cent of my time is spent on it. It is paperwork to do with prisoners, but there is nothing like getting round, you know. The problems are written down, but not dealt with. It would be actually better to spend more time with them and sort out the problems. It's all Home Office rulings – just building and building and building. (Prison Officer 9 – female)

There is infinitely more paperwork. One of the paradoxes of the past seventeen years is that there was a government elected that was going to trim the state, but in fact it has disbanded the state and perhaps undersold it. But all this about cutting out bureaucracy! In fact the amount of paper on the Probation Service has increased a thousandfold. We've had seventeen years of this business management culture transposed to something where it isn't necessarily applicable. I'm not saying people should be slipshod, unaccountable, shoddy. But I don't think that the sort of management ethos that is applicable to a ball-bearing factory is necessarily applicable to the Health Service or a prison. (Probation Officer 1 – male)

The paperwork is killing the job off. You want to do so much, but the paperwork means that you're snookered. (Prison Officer 13 – male)

I certainly think that some of the paperwork could be looked at. We're not just duplicating, we triplicate, and that's ridiculous. And just a little bit of consultation from headquarters before they introduce things? You tend to have people who plan these things and introduce them, send out all the

instructions and then suddenly you're backtracking on your-
selves because you can see that it's just not going to work. It
looks beautiful on paper, but you actually try and implement
it, it's not so easy. Now, surely the policies that are being
made at headquarters should be filtered down to us? And
that is what we've asked for. 'Please come and speak to us.
Please come and tell us what your policies are. Don't just fax
us something saying, "Read Instruction 9 of 84, or whatever,
and that will explain things". Sir David [Chief Inspector] has
spent a lot of time here and it gave me the opportunity to
talk to him. But I've sat up here with the Inspectorate team
before, and said the same type of thing, and there hasn't
been very much change, to be quite honest. (Prison Officer 6
– female)

One reason why Prison Headquarters do not explain exactly
what is required might be that they want to shift blame for
ineffective (or catastrophic) interpretations on to Governors. In
fact, of course, and as was argued above, discretion to interpret
rules is usually a sign that an agent or officer of the state has
been accorded the responsibility pertaining to her or his level of
competency. However, in a 'blame culture' it can also mean that
(s)he will be the only one for the high jump if anything goes
wrong. It can also result in officials at risk becoming more and
more restrictive in their interpretation and enforcement of
rules, as well as for a great deal of variation in interpretation
if the various officials assess the degrees of risk involved differently. To those whose lives the rules affect most closely,
rule variation can cause a great deal of anxiety and pain,
while campaigning groups become more and more impatient
with the disarming plethora of words masking a disappointing
paucity of deeds.

There's a ton of paper and a million words. There's paper on
this and policy on that. I can't bear to hear any more on prisoner rights, and prisoner accountability. *Because prisons are as
capricious as they ever were.* (Chris Tchaikovsky, Women in
Prison)

Prisoners themselves complained bitterly that so much that was
important to them had to be conducted paper to paper rather
than face to face:

Everything has to be through apps. [written applications], you know. I even had to put in an app. to get my release date. You practically have to put in an app. to go to the toilet. (Carol, aged 37)

But it was the variation in relation to the Incentives and Earned Privileges Scheme that caused most frustration, both for governors and prisoners. Different prisons applied different entry rules to the schemes – at one prison all new prisoners started on the Basic regime, at others all began on Standard. Sometimes, prisoners who have been transferred to another prison have to begin working their way up all over again. Small wonder that prisoners call the Basic, Standard and Enhanced Regimes Scheme 'BSE' – Mad Cow Disease.

We have Basic, two Standard and Enhanced and they come in at the lowest Standard – Standard 1 – which gives them spending power but not the community visits, when they're taken out with friends and family for six hours within a twenty mile radius. (Prison Officer 8 – female)

We don't have Basic, because my view is that anybody who is on basic shouldn't be here [open prison]. (Governor No 4 – male)

There's a national framework, but it's still up to what each prison can provide, and down to interpretation. It's always going to be like that. (Governor No 5 – male)

When I was in Holloway, I was on Enhanced and I was a Red Band as well, but when I came here I had to start again. And then in Holloway it is a privilege to be Enhanced and you can buy Body Shop stuff and things like that. But here if you're Enhanced, you're just Enhanced, they've got no incentive to give. (Amanda, aged 48)

A Governor agreed that if standards are being talked about, and especially in relation to incentives and privileges, they should indeed be standardized between prisons:

At the moment it is down to individual governors. But it is the sort of issue that I would have thought would benefit from at least thinking about a coordinated strategy. (Governor No 4 – male)

Another common complaint from staff and prisoners in some gaols was that either there were too few incentives attached to the Enhanced Regimes, or that the proffered incentives were not ones that women cared about. As one Board of Visitors' member put it, 'What's the good of holding out a fancy shampoo to them when their main worry is about their families?' Or, as a prisoner put it, just as realistically:

> If you're homeless and on drugs you're not going to mind losing a few days so long as you can still get stuff [illicit drugs] in here. A lot of the petty rules penalize those who just want to get on with their sentence, but make no difference to the girls who're in and out all the time. (Brenda, aged 32)

Yet, whatever flaws there are in the Incentives and Earned Privileges Scheme, it certainly is used as another weapon in the armoury of regulatory controls available to prison officers, and further subverts the idea that people go to prison *as* punishment rather than *for* punishment. One prison officer told me that he thought the standards of behaviour expected of women in prison were far too high, while more than one simply said, 'Men just wouldn't put up with the pettiness.' Others thought that for women who already have all kinds of problems the fear of regime demotion destructively adds yet another dimension of terror, 'and their behavioural problems just get worse'. Overall, many governors and officers implied that in the context of the all-pervasive and corrosive effects of the budgetary and staffing cuts of recent years, it was very difficult to claim that any one of the regime innovations which had added so much paperwork to the staff task had added equally to the quality of life of women prisoners.

BUDGETARY AND STAFFING CUTS

> Because of finances it is sometimes difficult getting materials replaced – whose budget will they come out of? Last year I had a couple of lawnmowers pack up. I only managed to keep them running because I had a car thief working for me. Because she was a car thief, she knew about engines. (Prison Officer 22 – male)

There have been developments, but the resources are not there to implement them. (Probation Officer 4 – female)

Something that's happened in most prisons is that any innovations that have been introduced have been drawn back because of budget cuts. The evening classes in education have all but disappeared, you know, not just recreational classes but instructional classes. Basically, that's all down to money. So any innovations you had in the early 1990s are disappearing from 1996 onwards because of cash restraints. (Prison Officer 6)
Carlen: Does that make your job more difficult?
Prison Officer 6: Females tend to just accept it, don't they? They just tend to accept it.

This year we had £350,000 cut off our operating budget. There is no budget for staff training any more. We're presently 8 prison officers short. (Prison Officer 13 – male)

We've had our budget and staff cut as our numbers have gone up. Now, in normal, sensible working conditions you would have expected more money to keep them and more staff to look after them. But in reality what's happened is that the population and the budget have gone in opposite directions. (Governor No 6)

We have two hundred and eighty prisoners but only purposeful work and activity for two hundred and twenty. We need another workshop, but we have no funds to have another workshop. It's all a knock-on effect of money and budgets. (Prison Officer 8 – female)

It can prevent you doing your job, because you'll go asking for something and there's no money in the budget. Simple as that. Doesn't matter if it's going to help them [prisoners] or not. (Prison Officer 9 – female)

We have reams and reams of paper, like snow, but if we have a cutback in staff which is the way it is going, then you're spending so much time doing paperwork that you're not spending time with them. We are allocated personal officer time, *if staffing permits, if staffing permits*. Other than that you're doing it on an evening duty. It's bad, it's really stretching staff at times, especially if you want to do quality work with them, which is what inmate development is.

You're struggling for staff all the time. The Government's cutting costs without basically understanding what prisons are all about, what we are trying to do. We actually, here, are trying to rehabilitate them. If it works with one in a hundred you've achieved something. (Prison Officer 2 – female)

Sentence Planning is a good idea but at the moment it is a bit of a paper exercise as we can't actually offer these courses that people want to go on, you know, anger management, drugs counselling, all that kind of thing. At the moment, we can say that we identify their need – we can do that easily. But then I'm afraid we can't actually supply something to satisfy the need. You would need a prison psychologist and resources that we just don't have. There are organizations that would willingly come and help, but they would also have to be paid and we haven't got the resources for that. (Prison Officer 15 – male)

Staff training was cut to the point where it was nil. Also, there's staff here with so many skills that are just not utilized because we haven't got the funding. We've got pre-release staff trained up but we don't do pre-release because we've not got the funds to put it on. (Prison Officer 11 – female)

Sentence Planning is taken seriously, but we just haven't got the time and staff to do it. They say we must do it, but when it comes down to staffing, you know, we just don't get the people. I would certainly like to see far more training for anger management, drug-related things, but everyone is governed by a budget now, and we just haven't got the money or the staff. I mean last year, they were running cookery classes, and they had to stop because they ran out of money. The Governor has got to save on the budget so he's looking at cutting back on things like probation and education. So, on the one hand, we must rehabilitate through education and probation, on the other hand we've got to cut their budgets back! So it's sort of robbing Peter to pay Paul (Prison Officer 16 – male)

Sentence Planning was a laudable idea and works to some extent, but there are so many competing priorities, that staff feel as if they're stretched to the ultimate in trying to complete all this work. It is quite one-to-one oriented and it does require a lot of time. One of the changes in the sentence management

programme is that we will be audited on it. In other words we
will be seen to have to produce figures about how much we are
doing, so we will be measured, certainly in the paper work
we will be measured. Now whether that paperwork exercise actually transposes into actions will depend upon us as a
management team. (Prison Officer 10 – female)

The prison will welcome ideas from main grade oficers, but
whether they'll institute them depends on funds. Everything
is down, unfortunately, to finances. We'd like to go to [names
other women's prisons] and see how they run things, so we
could generalize things, make sure that they get the same
things in each prison. But the old guard just think it would be
a day out. So no funds. (Prison Officer 1 – female)

Staff morale is a bit low. It's the Government trying to save
money, isn't it? (Prison Officer 4 – female)

If you're saving 17 per cent on what was already a very sparse
budget and the only thing you've got to play with is staff,
because that's what your major expenditure is, then there's
been a reduction to what many of my colleagues would say,
and I would agree with them, is a cut below safety levels.
(Governor No 2 – female)

Holloway? They just didn't have enough bodies there. They
can't unlock you, they say, because there's just not enough
staff to supervise. They've got a really good education thing,
that's if you're unlocked long enough to go. But then you
don't know if you're going to get your lesson every day. That's
the worst bit. (Carol, aged 37)

All the staff, in every prison I visited, mentioned the budgetary
restraints presently affecting all prisons. Individual staff in
some prisons went further, however, and contended that women
prisoners tend to lose out in the distribution of prison
resources. Some asserted that this was so whatever prison a
woman was in. Others claimed that women in shared site (male
and female) establishments were especially disadvantaged
when it came to sharing out the available funds.

When I came here I had never worked in a women's prison
before, and what struck me was that they have so little
compared with male prisoners. The men wouldn't put up

with it. (Prison Officer 13 – male in closed prison in North of England)

The women here are getting nothing. They need all kinds of things, psychologists, someone to talk to. It's because women don't cause much trouble. Men wouldn't put up with it. I wish you could get us some help. (Prison Officer 24 – male in closed prison in South of England)

Our gym is appalling compared to the men's side and our facilities aren't geared at all towards women. They knew that we were going to have women in plenty of time, they told us they would prepare for it. But I think we are the poor relatives, to be honest. (Prison Officer 17 – female, shared site establishment 1)

They've only got to have a member of staff short on the male side, and they've got a 'big crisis' meeting. But they are not interested in the crises we've got here. For instance, if they have to lock up the male side for a full day, that would be a big crisis. But if they have to lock up the female wing, that's not such a big deal... If the female estate wasn't marginalized in the way it is, we would have constructive activity instead of cutting probation services and no extra staff to deal with welfare problems. For instance, the men get the opportunity to cook food, they're given the better portions and quality. Another 'for instance', is that the male side have a hairdressing salon where the men can go and get qualifications, and they have an activity centre where they can do numerous things, like tiling and plastering. The women have none of that.

All the nightwear that is issued are pyjamas and they are male pyjamas! There's no nighties. So you could end up with a female who's been abused and raped wearing a pair of pyjamas that a sex offender could have had on – they have the fly-hole in and everything. Very undignified. (Prison Officer 11 – female, shared site establishment 2)

With that last example in mind, it may now be appropriate to close this chapter by examining the extent to which the emerging recognition by prison managers that the management requirements and personal needs of women prisoners are indeed different to those of male prisoners was, in 1997, already being realized in female prison regimes which might actually be seen as being more 'womenwise' than 'male stream'. For what is at stake is not some simplistic demand of equality for women prisoners – especially if prison equality means 'pie and chips' for everyone – regardless of women's different attitudes to food and diet; or if in practice it turns out that 'equality is male-pyjama-shaped'! What is at stake involves a politics of gender, race and class which has both institutional and jurisprudential ramifications. The jurisprudential dimensions will be dealt with in Chapter 4. This chapter will conclude with some reminders of why it is so important that the prison authorities in the future pay greater attention to the significance of gender differences than they have appeared to do in the recent past.

WOMEN'S IMPRISONMENT AND THE POLITICS OF DIFFERENCE

Interviews with the staff of the women's prisons made it very apparent that, throughout the women's prison sector there is a strong awareness that women's imprisonment is different from men's for three main reasons: biological – women's physical needs are essentially different to men's; social – women's role in the family is different to men's; and cultural – women's experiences of imprisonment are different to men's and have different meanings attached to them by both the women themselves and all those for whom, subsequently, they become 'prisoners' or 'ex-prisoners'.

At the same time, it will also have become very apparent that it can still be claimed that, despite all the concerned Inspectors' Reports and Prison Headquarters' agonizing about women prisoners' special needs, the female establishments in 1997 had not even begun to take seriously women's difference. Leaving aside the continuing inferior amenities in the women's establishments as compared with the men's; leaving aside too the crass 'across the board' implementation of Michael Howard's new security measures as a result of problems in the men's system; and postponing for the moment the vexed issue of requiring sentence differentiation on the grounds of pregnancy, motherhood or gender (an issue that will be dicussed in Chapter 4); in

1997 there was still no holistic approach to the basic issue of the operationalizing of regime and security concepts in a women-friendly fashion; and an almost complete avoidance of the issue of women, gender, identity and *sexuality*.

Penal Concepts and The Gender Test

Throughout this book – up to this point, at least – there has been an emphasis on the different social role of women within the family – on the set of expectations about women's proper place in the family which can materially affect women's experiences of imprisonment even when they may not have, in fact, been living out the conventional roles of mothers, wives and daughters before they went into prison. This focus on familiness does not only reflect the concerns of the women prisoners, it also mirrors the main thrust of most of the critical Reports. However, women in prison have concerns other than those which can be attributed to their domestic and family roles. They are also concerned about their citizenship-influenced claims for equality of rehabilitative opportunity with men. For their gender-influenced claims concerning recognition of their female identities and sexuality, also entail recognition that their citizen claims to dignity and respect may require realization in regimes and practices that are different to those most suitable for men. I am, therefore, arguing that, in future, all regime changes should be submitted to the 'gender test', a test asking whether biological or ideological differences in gender-identity will require proposed regime innovations to receive differential implementation in the men's and women's prisons. (Most likely similar arguments could be made that all regime innovations should be submitted to an 'ethnicity' test, though space does not allow for that argument to be made separately here. See Chiquada (1997) for a description of the experiences of black women in the criminal justice system, and Heaven (1996) for the experiences of foreign national women). That such a gender testing of regime and security innovations has not been routinely undertaken at the planning and inception stages was, in 1997, very evident from examples given to me by the prison staff themselves:

> Mandatory drug testing was an example of a complete lack of thought. When it was introduced nobody gave a thought that

women do it [urinate] differently to men. And we had to work out a different method of collection than occurred in the male prisons. It's a much more sensitive issue. (Governor No 4 – male)

We make the same mistake each time – the fighting that goes on just to say, 'Hang on these are women', you know? Take the mandatory drugs testing policy. 'This is what you do'. And we had to say, 'You can't say that to women, because they don't stand up and wee against the wall in front of other women, you'll have to do this differently. (Probation Officer 4 – female)

The concepts of dynamic security and volumetric control of property were also mentioned as requiring differential implementation according to gender. When dynamic security was discussed, arguments were repeatedly made that the women's prisons had, in any case, previously relied much more on dynamic security than the men's and that recent administrative changes had gone some way to eroding the good relationships based on trust which had traditionally been fostered in the women's prisons:

There was a time in the eighties when women became much more integrated with the male system, and we lost what was known as P4 which was the Headquarters organization that looked after women offenders. When they integrated the male and female systems they didn't look at what was working well in the female system and say, 'Let's adopt that for the males'. Instead they tended to overlay the male Service on to the female Service, and we lost some of the good stuff, like the particularly good relationships the prison officers had with the women. (Governor No 2 – female)

As for volumetric control, the *Thematic Review* (HM Chief Inspector 1997b) summarized very succinctly what prison staff emphasized to me at length:

The volumetric control policy was written with the property needs of the majority of prisoners, who are men, in mind. The result reflects insufficient account being taken of women's needs, for example, the volumetric control list used is written with 'he' and 'his' throughout and is clearly exactly

ne list used on the men's side. The national policy on
etric control... exempts one set of clothing worn by the
ler 'whether or not the prisoner wears own clothes' ...
from the total quantity of property which must fit into two
standard issue boxes. The policy is implemented to the disadvantage of women prisoners. (HM Chief Inspector of Prisons
1997b:52)

But, you may say, the fact that there *was* such a wide-ranging
review in 1997, and one, moreover, which obviously took gender
difference seriously, will surely put an end to gender-blindness
in relation to prison policy? One might hope so. However, in
1997 I still saw notices in some shared-site women's prisons
which referred to prisoners by the male pronoun – this one on
anti-bullying policy being typical:

If any prisoner is suspected of bullying, *he* will be charged...
(My emphasis)

Nitpicking? No. The point is this: ensuring that the language of
documents is gender-appropriate should be the *easiest* part of
what, when it comes to operationalizing gender-equality, is
inevitably a very complex process. Lack of attention to this
least difficult but most visible of gender issues is, unfortunately,
not suggestive of there being greater gender-sensitivity in the
areas which are much more difficult to analyze and address. So,
depressing as all this is, it is difficult to envisage anything other
than a very hit and miss policy on the recognition of gender differences until gender-awareness is incorporated centrally into
all prison personnel training, rather than being tagged on as an
'on the job' training afterthought for men about to work in a
women's prison for the first time. For, although the new induc-
tion course for men going to work in women's prisons is to be
welcomed, a majority of the men whom I interviewed in 1997
had still had no special training for working in a women's gaol
at all.

I was asked if I wanted to be Governor of X [women's] prison,
and in my career plan I'd never thought of going into a
women's prison. When it was offered me I thought, 'Well, I
can't think why I shouldn't'. But there was no training, no
preparation – except what I did myself. (Governor No 5 –
male)

The Governor is an extremely experienced governor who was very honest when he came here and said he hadn't got a clue about women's prisons. But no-one sat him down and said, 'This is what you need in terms of operating a women's prison'. (Probation Officer 4 – female)

Some women officers complained that once females had started working in a women's establishment, it was difficult to make the move to the male sector, primarily because the women's institutions are not popular with female officers.

I've been in the Service eleven years and I would like to move on to working with male prisoners to enhance my career. But I am penalized from doing so because there are not enough females who want to work in the female estate. I am discriminated against because of my gender, because they can't get anyone to work with these women. (Prison Officer 11 – female)

Worse, many officers, both men *and* women, felt that there was some kind of professional stigma attached to working in the women's establishments. At worst, the sense of stigma could affect an officer's career prospects.

Working in the women's sector has been seen as being a bit isolated, and people haven't felt it was a good career. (Governor No 7 – male)

At a more personal level, it was suggested that some women officers were now very reluctant to be forced to carry out intrusive security measures – like mandatory drug testing or strip searching – on other females. At the level of job satisfaction, the day-to-day work experience could be adversely affected by the general resource disadvantages suffered by the women's prison estate. Most irritatingly for male personnel, a job in the women's prisons could be seen by other men in the Service as being a bit of a laugh, not a real job for a man at all!

My regional director would have a smile on his face whenever he came to see me when I was Governor of Y [women's prison]. He thought it was a big giggle. That was the level at which those issues [women's prisons in general, lesbianism in particular] were being dealt with. Not in terms of professionalism. The Prison Service should be ensuring that prison staff can talk openly about all those issues. Senior managers are not prepared for these issues, nor, for God's sake, is there any mechanism for even talking about them in a supported way. (Male ex-governor of a women's prison)

And I would argue that, despite the lip-service which has now been paid to gender issues by the Prison Service for at least a couple of years, it is unlikely that there will be any effective support mechanism for prison staff troubled by women and gender issues until there is a holistic approach to the theorizing of penality and gender difference; together with a gender-testing of all new regime innovations.

Gender, Sexuality and The Politics of Difference

The recent official discovery of gender issues in women's prisons has, as I have indicated in previous pages, concentrated on those gender issues traditionally associated with maternity, nurturance of the young and weak, and domesticity. There has been a silence about gender, sexuality and penality. Yet sexuality figured frequently in the discourses of both staff and prisoners as they talked about the main causes for concern in the women's establishments. With prisoners the emphasis tended to be on the nature of the sexual gaze and the unease they experience in having males working in their living quarters, though one female officer also expressed concern about the failure of male officers to contextualize women's behaviour either in terms of the physical changes occasioned by the menstrual cycle or in terms of their previous sexual histories:

Cross sex posting, which is males and females working with opposite sexes, can have a calming influence on each sex, but [when it comes to male officers working in a female establishment] if you go to bed you want to go to bed with no underwear on, and the fact that during the night you could kick off the covers and a male patrol could come and look through the hatch (with the best intentions, to make sure you are safe and OK) – but you're exposed and could be sat on the toilet seat – and a male officer walks in! If *I* walk into a room and a woman's on the toilet I feel embarrassed, so I know how the woman feels.

When I deal with a woman, if she's a bit off with me, I think, 'Is she PMTing?' But men don't seem to be sensitive to this kind of thing. One male [officer] had a lot of toiletries taken off an inmate and put into property, and when I came on duty the girl was in tears – she was forever buying soap, bubble bath and skin cleaners and that kind of thing. When I realized she was doing this, the first thing I said was, 'Has she been abused? Has she been raped?' And she had. (Prison Officer 11 – female)

Prisoners were always careful to say that they did not object to men *per se* working in the prisons. What they were primarily concerned about was that they could be kept under surveillance by men in the most intimate details of their daily lives, including times when they were either naked (when they were washing) or when they were engaged in performing bodily functions which conventionally (in the world beyond the prison walls) are required to be completed in private.

I've no objection to the employment of men in the prison. In some ways it's quite good. Nice to have some male conversation now and then. But I do object when two men do the patrols on the houses at night. Especially at four o'clock in the morning, they either tip the curtain back and shine a torch in, or they actually walk into the room. I don't like that. It could be very awkward. (Amanda, aged 48)

One of my favourite officers is a male officer, and in my experience – you know when they are going to come into your room. But a lot of people find it distressing because they could be bathing – if you're, like, Asian, you could find it distressing. (Ruth, aged 18)

In single cells here there's no curtains, nothing to shield the toilet. They can look in and see you straight away. Fair enough, we've done wrong and we're in prison; but we don't need to be treated like animals. (Liz, aged 19)

If you've got a single cell and the toilet is there, if they open your door they can see you. That, I think is the worst bit. I couldn't care less if they saw me with no clothes on, but watching you go to the toilet is a different matter, isn't it? (Carol, aged 37)

Women don't feel safe with males on overnight. We've had this complaint again and again. They don't think it's right that male prison officers should unlock women, should have 24 hour surveillance so they can see them on the toilet or getting undressed. (Chris Tchaikovsky, Women in Prison)

Next to the shower room – it has a very thin shower curtain – is a hot water machine and the men prison officers come down there to get their tea. They're stood there getting their drink and they can see through the curtain while you are in the shower. That's not very nice. (Kay, aged 46)

The men are very good, but I don't agree with men coming on the houses at night because they look into your rooms. Most of the time I get very tired and the last check is between nine and half past to make sure you're in your room, and I'm usually in bed, sometimes asleep, and sometimes it's two men and they actually come into your room, to make sure you are there. And I think they should have women to do that. (Jan, aged 44)

Many women always tried to dress themselves behind the door at opening times, because although all male officers were supposed to knock on the doors and say, 'Are you decent?' before they came in, one male officer in particular never knocked. (Claire, aged 37)

They can look through the peephole. It made me feel very uncomfortable. There's no curtains, not even round the bloody toilet! If you're sitting on the toilet and a man opens the door, I think it's terrible. (Jill, aged 45)

Also to do with women's sexuality was the awareness that some prisoners, because they had been victims of male sexual or physical abuse, were even more sensitive to male officers being at large in their living quarters:

We have quite a few [inmates] that come in and have had violent partners and they've got a thing against men. Plus sometimes we could end up with six male staff on the wing with one female on an evening. Now I myself wouldn't like to have to ask a man for a tampax or a sanitary towel. We had an instance when a woman asked one of the male staff for a sanitary towel and he went away and brought a Lillet back

and gave it to her, and she said, 'I can't wear one of then.
and he said, 'Of course you can, it's for the same thing'. And
he didn't know the difference, that some people cannot physically wear something without any applicator, you know? It
just shows you how naive some of the men are. (Prison
Officer 11 – female)

Not a *sexual* issue, it may be objected. But by many of the
women who talked about these issues to me they *were* seen as
sexual issues. They objected to having to talk to males about
matters of female hygiene that they did not talk to *anybody*
about outside prison; and they resented being obliged to name
body parts (that they usually only discussed and clinically
referred to with their doctors) to male gaolers who had no
medical qualifications at all.

None of the prisoners I interviewed reported that male
officers were abusing their positions of trust by becoming sexually involved with women, though prison managers readily dis-
closed the information that some male officers had been
disciplined for unprofessional conduct with inmates. By and
large, however, the view of the women prisoners on the issue of
illicit liaisons between staff and prisoners was that 'it takes two
to tango':

> They don't harass anyone, but some do play around with
> women who come on to them. One woman I know, she was
> being felt up by a male officer in the cell. But she didn't
> mind. Men will be men sometimes, and though they know
> what the risks are, some can't see as far as their fucking
> noses. They'll take the risk. (Deborah, aged 31)

Women prisoners' primary concern, therefore, was not whether
male staff would sexually molest them or behave unprofession-
ally. It was that all prison staff in the normal course of their
duties are licensed to gaze on women's bodies and that prisoners
have no control whatsoever over the guardianship of what,
outside prison, would be considered to be not only their most
private parts, but also their most private moments. This cannot
be stressed enough; for I am not convinced that all prison personnel appreciate that what is at stake here (from the female
prisoners' standpoint) is the sexual abuse of repressive power –
rather than merely that of staff professionalism.

ussed the issue of women prisoners' fears of the
ırient gaze in terms of officer professionalism,
professional prison officers do not ogle women
ittingly happen upon in a state of undress. So
, male officers do strip-searching and MDT, and all
officers, especially male officers knock on the doors of women's
cells, then, they claimed, there is no cause for concern. These
points were made by staff at all levels, and were summed up by
one very eloquent male governor who said:

> The important point is to get men in who are good role
> models, because a lot of these women have never met a
> decent man or a man who can keep his trousers zipped up.
> You know what I mean? Those are the key things. Because
> they've often seen men as predators, or as oppressors, or as
> bullies, and actually need to meet some reasonable men. We
> never have more than one man on at night, and he is sup-
> ported by female staff. Men – well, all staff – are directed to
> knock before they go into rooms unless there is a security
> consideration. Then, prisoners have said to me that it's just
> as bad to have a dyke or lesbian officer barge in, or to have
> lesbian officers strip-searching. But I don't think there's any
> way round that. Obviously we won't have men strip-searching
> them! But yes, they do have an inhibition of going to male
> officers and asking for sanitary towels and things like that.

Sensitive as these comments are, it is my argument that they
miss the point. The women themselves expressed less concern
that they would be raped by male officers or eyed-up by lesbians
and more concern about the violation of the social convention
that dictates that women should usually take pains to hide their
sexual parts from all but their chosen sexual partners or a
medical practitioner. Exposure to either of these categories of
inspection is usually (or ideally) assumed to be voluntary. But
when a woman is forced to expose her body (in a strip search),
to engage in supervised urinating (in the MDT test), or to live
in constant fear that she will be involuntarily exposed to the
surveillance of a prison officer (male or female) who may or
may not look upon her with the gaze of a voyeur – but who will
certainly look upon her with a legitimated punitive stare – it is
arguable that she, sensing a perversion of both legitimate punishment and legitimate sex, will feel an intense humiliation.

For although there is a silence about the numbers of lesbian officers working in the women's prisons, their visibility to the prisoners makes them an easy target for the displacement of the women's more general fears of sexual vulnerability – as Karen made evident:

> In the mornings, male officers would come in, and they can look through and see what you are doing. But the women worried me just as much, because you didn't know whether they were gay or straight. I've got nothing against men or gay people, but when you are in that situation you know that they've got total control. (Karen, aged 21)

That is the nub of the matter – the vulnerability of women prisoners' naked bodies or exposed sexual parts to the possible lusts, derision or merely coldly casual inspections of their gaolers – whether those gaolers be male or female, heterosexual or lesbian. It is not a new problem, it is basic to all women's prison regimes, and, again, it is one that was brought to the attention of the public in the second decade of the century.

> Our evidence indicates that little attention is paid to the special needs of women during their monthly periods... The complaint is also made that proper privacy is not afforded. We take the following statement from the speech of an ex-prisoner at a conference arranged by the Prison Reform League in June, 1917:
>> Owing to prison negligence I became ill and only left my cell for four hours' exercise on four different days – during the whole of my sentence. My cell was, therefore, my dining room, my bedroom, my bathroom and my water closet. I must of course leave a good deal to your imagination, but can you realise what it meant when the male governor, male deputy governor, male doctors, male chaplains, male visiting magistrates, male inspector, all apparently have the right to plunge into your cell-bedroom without the slightest warning, or even knocking, or even asking your permission ... I do not want to labour the point, but I say there is not one woman in this audience – whether single or married – who would like to think that any strange man could burst into her bedroom in this way.
> (Hobhouse and Brockway 1922:345)

And that heartfelt protest makes no mention of strip-searching – and was written well before the advent of mandatory drug testing and cross-gender postings for prison officers! Yet, as has been suggested in the previous pages of this book, despite the persistence of certain features which are integral to the logic of imprisonment, women's prisons are constantly changing, both cosmetically and in their penal effects, to meet both political pressures and populist demands.

During the last decade of the twentieth century the two main political imperatives in criminal justice matters have been that more offenders should be seen to be receiving tough custodial sentences and that (as back-up to the harsher sentencing policies) the regimes in all prisons should be organized to maximize prisoners' pain. The main argument in this chapter has been that as a result of the overlaying of penal repression with a fetishized bureaucratic surveillance, both of which have been designed and implemented with a manifest disregard for biological and gender differences between men and women, end-of-century innovations in sentencing and imprisonment in England have impacted more painfully and inappropriately on women than on men.

In relation to the use of imprisonment in general, it is time to admit that prison does *not* work (in terms of reducing crime – see Howard League 1993; Currie 1996; Hale 1998), and that there is, as the twenty-first century approaches, a much more urgent need to regulate crime control itself (see Morgan and Carlen 1998).

With reference to the quality of contemporary penal control, it should be noted that in overlaying penal repression with the trappings of bureaucratic legitimacy, politicians have ensured that prisoners are nowadays not only secured in gaol under repressive conditions, but that they are being further humiliated by being forced to collude in their own repression. (I think in particular of prisoners having the relevant regulation read to them before being made to urinate under supervision; and of being required to engage in 'sentence planning' with an officer who may also strip them, watch them urinate, and then plan with them the enforced removal of their infant children from the prison at the age of 9 or 18 months. But other examples could be given.) In short, it is also time we recognized that the old adage that 'offenders go to prison *as* punishment and not *for* punishment' is misleading nonsense. Recent Home Secretaries have introduced measures designed to ensure not only that prisoners are kept securely in custody, but also that they find the actual prisons unpleasant places. In the case of most women prisoners, several distinctive dimensions of their imprisonment render it arguable that present 'policies' on the penal control of women are absurd. Taken together, they help constitute a penal sledgehammer which batters female offenders with an incremental and gendered punishment which, in the vast majority of cases, is either out of all proportion to the gravity (or rather, lack of gravity) of their crimes, or inappropriately unmindful of the wider implications of women's imprisonment. Chapter 4 will discuss whether or not this destructive sledgehammer can be replaced by more productive ways of responding to women's crimes.

4 The Futures of Women's Imprisonment

It is December 16th, 1997. I think of the imprisoned mothers who, because they are in gaol for a relatively minor crime, won't be with their children this Christmas. I think, too, of the young girls who have already spent most of their childhoods in institutions, and who will this year be locked up in a prison cell for much of Christmas Day.

Last week the government initiated legislation for a reduction in the welfare benefits of single parents. Yesterday, I received a communication from the Prison Reform Trust asking for a subscription to help fund an 'independent inquiry' into women's imprisonment. This morning a researcher from Probation phoned for advice on how to investigate the needs of women newly released from gaol. Bit by bit the welfare state is being dismantled. Year by year more and more women are being sent to prison. (There may not be a connection, though much research suggests that there is.) The reports and books detailing the waste of women's imprisonment pile higher and higher. To no effect. There *must* be an alternative. (Author's diary, 16 December 1997)

The women's system has no management strategy. Governors are nervy about women's prisons. There is no structure and strategy on which they can hold. Men or women working in the female establishments are not highly regarded. No-one on the present prison Board has knowledge of women prisoners.

The Prison Service is used by Society as a sump and has no answers of its own. There is no analysis of the resources needed to run it properly. It is a myth that it is about crisis and only about crisis. The problem is that the Department only knows how to play it on the back foot. If it hasn't a crisis, it has to create one. It's only in crisis that it feels alive. It needs to be in a healthy state but the Prison Service acts out the disorder of the client. (Senior Official in the Home Office)

This chapter discusses three possible futures for women's imprisonment. On the basis of the research findings presented and the arguments made in the previous pages, the critical thrust is predicated upon two assumptions: that prison does *not* work; and that the social meanings and jurisprudential implications of women's imprisonment are significantly different to those of men's. The chapter is therefore divided into three sections, subtitled as follows: (1) Prison does not work; (2) Women's imprisonment – the jurisprudential questions; and (3) The futures of women's imprisonment.

PRISON DOES NOT WORK

> Prison is obviously a destructive experience. Therefore the best the regimes can do is try to ameliorate the worst effects. Despite all this 'prison works' bollocks that we've had around for the last few years, prison is basically a destroyer. I mean, it [prison works] is a total lie, and to a gullible public who knows nothing about prisons, it just feeds prejudice. (Senior Official in the Home Office)

> There are not many people at headquarters who have actually worked in a women's prison, and there are even fewer who know anything at all about a women's open prison. So, we're on a hiding to nothing really. (Governor No 4 – male)

> I think that a lot of public opinion is dictated by the government – you know: 'Lock them up and lose the key'. But it doesn't work, it doesn't work. It's all very well saying that probation is a soft option, but, if prison's not working, you've got to try the alternatives. (Prison Officer 1 – female)

> We've got a thankless job, because we come to work and we're just holding people. It's like saying, 'Let's waste a year of somebody's life'. Say they get a two year sentence; they're either in the sewing shop or on a basic education course – we only run basic education here. They'll go out and they'll be put back in the same environment, knowing that they can't get a job because they've been in prison. I really can totally understand why they go back to crime. I know it's a terrible thing for a prison officer to say, but I really do understand

why they do it. They can't find a job, they've got little children to look after, they've got no money, and they see everybody else with money. It's very diffficult to know what to say
to them. You go home some days, and think,'Well, how the
hell have I helped anyone today?' (Prison Officer 14 – female)

There are supposed to be at least eight politico-philosphical
justifications for imprisonment:

- expiation: the state has an obligation to give malefactors the
  opportunity to pay for their crimes and thereby wipe the
  slate clean;
- reform: prisons can be used to improve people's characters;
- rehabilitation: prisons can teach people useful and new skills
  which will help them to lead law-abiding lives when they are
  released;
- retribution: the 'eye for an eye' philosophy that holds that
  the state has an obligation to citizens to impose as much pain
  on lawbreakers as they have already inflicted on their
  victims;
- denunciation: a society should incarcerate wrongdoers in
  order to show its abhorrence of particular crimes;
- general deterrence: the public knowledge that lawbreakers
  go to prison is supposed to deter others tempted to commit
  crime;
- individual deterrence: people sent to prison are thereby
  deterred from breaking the law in the future;
- incapacitation/public protection: the criminal is prevented
  from committting offences while incarcerated, the public is
  thereby protected and the crime rate lowered.

No shortage of justifications for imprisonment! Yet, many of
those listed above make ill-founded assumptions about the
effects of incarceration. Moreover, it might seem to a cynic
ruminating on the statistical findings of researchers attempting to investigate the validity of some of the claims concerning
the efficacy of imprisonment (see below), that maybe the main
political uses of, (as opposed to the classical justifications for),
the increased dependence on penal incarceration in recent
times, have been primarily activated by governments keen to
divert attention from certain other social problems (such as the
growing economic inequality which is much more threatening

to the legitimacy of governments) by whipping up a populist demand for a 'war on crime'. If that has indeed been the case, the resulting and intertwined spirals of fear of crime and more and more punitive sentencing will now only be broken and disentangled by a government honest enough to admit that prison does *not* work and sufficiently courageous to accept that prison is itself 'part of the crime problem, rather than part of the solution' (Prison Reform Trust 1993; see also, Worrall 1997). But let us not be cynical here. Let us, instead, examine the conventional justifications for imprisonment, and see if we can find out what Michael Howard could possibly have meant when he claimed that 'prison works'.

It is as unlikely that anyone at the end of the twentieth century is concerned about the religious notion that offenders should be given the chance to pay for their crimes by expiating them in prison as it is that anyone nowadays expects gaols either to reform or rehabilitate their inmates. 'Reform' (of prisoners' characters) went out of the window for good in 1988 when it was officially accepted that 'prisons make bad people worse' (Home Office 1988); while many liberal prison reformers (writing from an entirely different perspective on prisoners and imprisonment) had already undermined the plausibility of the 'rehabilitation' rhetoric by demonstrating (alternatively) that penal incarceration makes already-bad *situations* (outside prison) worse (eg Pitman and Gordon 1958; Davies 1974; Carlen *et al.* 1985). Lord Woolf (1991), as well as many good people working within the prison service, would still like to see prison regimes organized so that prisoners themselves are better equipped to lead good and useful lives when they are discharged. However, the combination of gaol overcrowding and the imposition of the new and increasingly restrictive security measures in the 1990s has resulted in many prison governors currently arguing that the most prisons can hope to achieve under present operating conditions is 'damage limitation'.

Certainly Mr Howard was correct to think that imprisonment is retributive. It does impose pain and deprivation on offenders, though, given the increasingly poor circumstances of many prisoners' lives outside gaol, it is most probably unwise to assume that the retributive intent of penal incarceration necessarily has deterrent effects on the individuals subjected to it. Likewise with denunciation. It is foreseeable that there will always be universally abhorred crimes against which a society will wish to take an ethical, retributivist and protectionist stance by imposing severe penalties on the perpetrators. In the absence of executions or banishment, moreover, those sanctions are likely to involve some kind of incarceration. But, as for the general deterrence effects of such denunciatory punishments...who knows? How can we ever come near to assessing what part the very existence of the criminal justice and penal systems play in keeping the rest of us on the straight and narrow? And though the relationships between incarceration and incapacitation may be more amenable to isolation, measurement and prediction than any that may exist between state punishment and general deterrence, it is still extremely difficult to gauge exactly what size of increase in the total numbers of lawbreakers in prison at any one time might actually reduce crime levels via incapacitation of sufficient proportions of all active criminals. Yet reduction of crime via the prison's deterrent and incapacitative effects is exactly what Howard was claiming for penal incarceration when he pronounced that:

> It [prison] ensures that we are protected from muggers and rapists, and it makes many who are tempted to commit crime think twice. (Michael Howard, Home Secretary 1993, reported in Prison Reform Trust 1993)

The logical arguments and statistical evidence against both justifications are substantial.

Claims that severe prison sentences deter either potential or recidivist offenders are based on the assumption that people rationally weigh the likely costs of crimes before committing them. There is no evidence to support this assumption. Most crimes are opportunistic, and experienced criminals contemplating a crime know that the risk of being caught and sent to prison is low. Michael Howard preferred to believe that if in fact imprisonment is not a deterrent to future offending it is either because prisons are too soft or that too few people are presently being gaoled. Yet, as the Prison Reform Trust has pointed out:

> Similar beliefs underpinned the 'short, sharp shock' experiment of the early 1980s ... It was the subject of a detailed evaluation study by the Home Office which found that it

neither deterred potential offenders nor influenced those who were subject to it. Reoffending rates reached eighty per cent within two years of discharge. There is little or no evidence that making the prison experience more punitive reduces prisoners' propensity to reoffend. (Prison Reform Trust 1993)

Furthermore, when this question of prison deterrence has been looked at from a different angle, there has been some slight support for the argument that although a term of imprisonment may make prisoners resolve never to get into criminal trouble again, whether or not they actually put the resolution into effect will be crucially determined by their employment and domestic circumstances upon release, with good accommodation, decent job and satisfying relationships being of prime importance (Carlen 1988). This is a research lead that might well repay further investigation.

The very complex question of whether prison reduces the overall crime rate by at least preventing offenders from committing crime while they are in custody has been investigated by Roger Tarling (1993) who at the time of the research was Head of the Home Office Research and Planning Unit. After extensive investigation and analysis Tarling concluded that:

> ... the incapacitation effect of current levels of imprisonment is not great... A general increase in the use of imprisonment, either by increasing the proportion sentenced to custody, increasing the sentences imposed or increasing the proportion of the sentence that offenders spend in custody, would not affect crime levels by any substantial amount. (Tarling 1993, quoted in Prison Reform Trust 1993)

Hale (1998), using econometric techniques to model trends in crime and punishment in England and Wales between 1950 and 1993 found no evidence that changes in the use of imprisonment had any impact on burglary levels.

WOMEN'S IMPRISONMENT – THE JURISPRUDENTIAL QUESTIONS

I can see that from the point of view of the judges they can't just say that because you're a woman you're not going to prison, because, you know, if you commit the crime, you should do the time. But I've not seen my child for ten months, it's a long time. I've lost my home – so I could end up losing everything. (Louise, aged 26)

Well, there are people who are in for petty, stupid crimes and if they've got a whole string of those 'taken into account', maybe it looks quite bad, and you think, 'Oh yes, send them away for a couple of years'. But then you realize that the children suffer so badly being separated from their mother. The women lose their jobs, their houses, they lose everything. You then think that maybe the punishment is out of proportion to the crime, and also the full cost of the punishment is out of all proportion, too. (Prison Officer 15 – male)

In my view, you need something – the political will to jerk the whole prison system out of its 'react to crisis' role. It won't happen, though, unless and until the prison system is seen as part of a partnership within the whole criminal justice and social services system, where the courts – to sort of put it simplistically – ought to be able to say to the prison service, 'We're sentencing this person to X sentence; we expect you to do this and this with this person'. (Senior Official in the Home Office)

The Question of Differential Sentencing

A difficult question confronting campaigners on women's prisons issues is: how can it be argued that fewer women should receive custodial sentences without it also being implied that there should be a sexist discrimination against men that would license women to break the law with impunity?

In reply to this question, one strategy has been to argue as follows: first, that the economic, ideological and political conditions in which women break the law are different to those in which men commit crime (Messerschmidt 1986; Carlen 1988); second, that women are already subject to a differential sentencing by the courts, the logic of which is seldom made explicit, and when it is, frequently appears to be rooted in oppressive and outmoded assumptions about the 'proper' role of women in society in general, and their 'proper' relationships with men in particular; and third, that in any case, women who appear before the courts usually suffer a discriminating double regulation because they will have already been subjected to innumerable 'anti-social' and informal controls (not suffered by their male counterparts) which will in turn have already atrophied their opportunities for full citizenship (Carlen 1995; Carlen and Tchaikovsky 1996).

There is abundant evidence to support those claims, and there is no doubt that criteria already come into play in the sentencing of women which are different to those employed in the sentencing of men. The implication of the foregoing arguments is this: that as women already suffer adverse social control in society at large (especially in disproportionately being victims of extreme poverty, sexual abuse and domestic violence), the courts would be justified in taking such gendered histories into account when passing sentence in individual cases. Even if it were difficult to argue in particular cases that the poverty or abuse suffered had had direct influence on the crime committed, they could still be taken into account if it could be argued that they had had an indirect influence; for example, if a young woman's criminal or drugs career had started after she had left home as a result of sexual or physical abuse.

Now, if at this point some readers are cynically thinking that anyone could make up apposite and excusing histories to avoid a custodial sentence, then I would say to them that they should peruse in all their horrifying detail some of the histories of young women in care or penal institutions. They are too often blood-chilling sagas of institutionalization (from birth), sexual and physical abuse, illness, bereavement, homelessness and poverty that do indeed go way beyond belief. In the vast majority of cases, however, they will not only be well-authenticated by a stack of social-work dossiers stretching back years, but also by the women's worn physical, and damaged, mental and emotional, states. Unless such women have committed very serious crimes (that merit a denunciatory sentence) or crimes that make them a danger to the public (and they therefore have to be incarcerated as a matter of public protection), no good can come of their being locked up. Almost certainly they will require help of some description – *but always of a kind that no prison can provide.* Imprisonment can only damage them further, and make them more likely to break the law in future.

The above arguments notwithstanding, it has to be admitted that whenever questions about women's imprisonment are raised in debate, even the most critical and informed commentators still express concern about the jurisprudential dilemmas inherent in any implication that women, *purely on grounds of their sex,* should be treated more leniently (either in the courts or the gaols) than men who commit similar crimes. Yet, the differentiated sentencing of defendants (found guilty of like crimes) according to their social circumstances is, in itself, not a new phenomenon, and has, at various times, actually been part of official policy, especially in relation to young people.

The practical difficulty of arguing nowadays for a reduction in the women's prison population solely on the basis of what little is known about present sentencing logic inheres not so much in a residual resistance to responding to similar crimes differently according to the sex of the offender, but in the impossibility of deducing from statistical analyses alone exactly why any prison population currently takes the form it does. (See Daly, 1994, and Howe 1994 for the complexities invoved in such analyses; see Hedderman and Gelsthorpe 1997 for a most recent and inconclusive attempt). There is, for instance, always the possiblity (and some evidence – see Carlen 1983, 1990) that a few paternalistic sentencers may actually think that they are reducing the misery of the most destitute women by 'sending them to prison to be looked after' (magistrate to author while both were visiting East Sutton Park Prison in 1997). Therefore, rather than attempting to delve into the 'truth' (of the murky logic) behind contemporary sentencing practices it might be more productive of a reduction in the female prison population merely to propose that, in the future, sentencers should be required (a) to justify (to a Sentencing Council) all custodial sentences and remands (for both men and women) in terms of their appropriateness to the offender, the offence and any pre-existing sentencing criteria for the award under scrutiny; (b) to make very explicit what they hope to achieve by the custodial sentence awarded; and (c) to make a calculation of what the *total* costs of the sentence are likely to be. (After all, the requirement of financial accountability is nowadays imposed on all other public servants. Why not make the same demands of sentencers?) The thinking behind this latter strategy is that if the courts are going to continue sending women (or men) to prison for trivial offences, they should publicize the financial and social costs of what they are doing, say what they hope to get for their money – and let the public also have a chance to count the costs of (too carelessly) assuaging its punitive urge. Adoption of this strategy would most likely reveal that more female than male prisoners are actually being sent to prison because, given their more complex histories of abuse, and mental and emotional disorders, no other institution will take them (Carlen, 1983; Maden *et al.* 1994). Being in the position of having to calculate and pronounce publicly on the costs of their own sentencing practices *might* also have the effect of shaming sentencers into demanding more appropriate ways of dealing with women (and men) whose primary problem is more medical or psychiatric than criminal.

The Question of Different Prison Regimes for Men and Women

> People are a bit wary of going down the road of making different rules for female prisoners. I do think that women in prison have different needs to men. I do think they bring more baggage into prison in so far as they have greater family responsibilities. And I do think that they are less of a security risk. But if we start saying, for example, that female prisoners can have trips home every six weeks to see the kids, then why shouldn't male prisoners, some of whom are also single parents, turn round and expect the same treatment? (Governor No 5 – male)

And the short answer is, 'Yes, why shouldn't they? And, if they did, why couldn't the same criteria be applied to their requests as to women's?' (For it was repeatedly put to me by staff in the women's establishments that, instead of all the 1990s security measures being imposed equally on the male and female gaol populations, more effort should have been expended on investigating whether there were any lessons to be learned from the women's prisons, many of which had practised various forms of 'dynamic security' for years.)

   The longer answer is that first, far fewer male prisoners are in the position of being sole carers for their children (see Home Office 1992a; and HM Chief Inspector of Prisons 1997b); and that, secondly, more would be disqualified on other grounds, for example longer and more serious criminal records (see Morris *et al.* 1995). That said (and in light of many of the comments made by prison staff quoted earlier in this book), it is difficult to see how it could be other than a progressive development for more male prisoners to be genuinely and responsibly concerned about, and involved in, the welfare of their families while they are serving their time. However, the main question here is whether the women's prisons should be run differently to the males, and, for all the reasons adduced in the last chapter, it is argued that they should be.

Throughout this book it has been demonstrated that the needs of female and male prisoners are different in many aspects and vary, also, according to age, sexual orientation, ethnicity, and other biographical detail, especially histories of institutionalization, abuse and illness. Though no institutional arrangements could ever be tailored to cater for the unique mix of each individual's requirements, the broad differences attributable to gender and ethnicity *can* be more easily catalogued and allowed for. Therefore, and as was argued in the last chapter, as part of a programme of 'ameliorative justice' in prisons, all aspects of prison life should be 'gender-tested' and 'ethnicity-tested' to ensure that general prison regulations, local rule interpretations and the different types of prison regimes do not, because of gender and/or ethnic differences, impact more harshly on certain groups of inmates than others. To engage in this type of discrimination in order to avoid imposing disproportionate pain on certain groups identifiable by either gender and/or ethnicity, would, far from being inequitable, help promote greater substantive equality between prisoners whose formal equality of custodial experience would otherwise be grossly undermined by the differential impact on it of gender and or ethnicity. It is for this reason, and building on the prison governors' concept of 'damage limitation', that I am proposing that an overall policy principle of 'ameliorative justice' should be used in conjunction with the gender-testing (and ethnicity- testing) of all new regime initiatives and security innovations, to assess whether or not the implementation of any proposed new regime or security features will disproportionately worsen the situation of women, men or specific ethnic minority groups in prison.

By using the term 'ameliorative justice', I am not invoking any notions of 'reform' or 'treatment' of prisoners – just the twofold notion that: first, as the confinement in itself is the punishment of the court, prison administrators should do everything in their power to limit the damage done by that penal confinement, especially any extra damage likely to be done by the prison regime because of a person's gender or ethnicity; and, secondly, and to avoid any 'levelling down' rather than 'levelling up' of damage limitation, that prison administrators should aim to achieve, through rule and regime variation, the most humane outcome for the greatest number of prisoners. If a combined system of ameliorative justice and gender-testing had been in place in the very recent past, several embarrassing and shameful scandals – for instance, manacling women in labour, forcing women never known to have taken drugs to urinate in full view of a prison officer, and requiring male officers to patrol the cells of female prisoners at night – might have been avoided. If gender-testing is not implemented in the future some new, and maybe worse, scandals can be expected in the women's prisons.

THE FUTURES OF WOMEN'S IMPRISONMENT

It is December 18th, 1997, and today I received the Chief Inspector's Report of the Inspection of Bullwood Hall Young Offender Institution (HM Chief Inspector of Prisons 1997c) which was published last week. The Inspection was undertaken in May this year. It is important to quote Sir David Ramsbotham's [Chief Inspector's] first few lines of the Preface to the Report – if only to make sure that more people, than might otherwise be the case, learn that the Prison Service has been told yet again that it is failing to give proper care and attention to the women's prison establishments. (Author's diary, 18 December 1997)

This report on HMP and YOI Bullwood Hall makes depressing reading, not only because of the story it tells but because, given proper care and attention by senior Prison Service management, it need never have happened. I have called over and over again for the Prison Service to appoint a Director of

Women because, in women's prison after women's prison, I find neglect of their needs...if senior managemment doubt the force of what I am saying, they should ask themselves why and how they allowed HMP Holloway, the women's wing at HMP Risley, the women's wing at HMRC Low Newton, the staffing at HMP Brockhill and now the problems of HMP and YOI Bullwood Hall not only to occur, but to continue, and why they have had to declare so many women's establishments in need of special attention... (HM Chief Inspector of Prisons 1997c:5)

The actual Report on HM Young Offender Institution Bullwood Hall made 186 recommendations. One of the most important was for the 'establishment of an integrated operational strategy and ethos for the treatment of female young offenders within which establishments should develop appropriate regimes' (HM Chief Inspector of Prisons 1997d:28).

It is obvious that an integrated management system for the women's prison estate must have a part to play in any holistic approach to the regulation of female offenders. But, as I wrote at the beginning of this book, it really is not much use piling blame on the Prison Service for the state of the women's prisons while they continue to be so overcrowded and under-resourced. Nor, moreover, is an integrated management system enough in itself. It needs to be based on sound principles relating both to women's difference from men, and also, (given the ethnic composition of the women's prison population) on a well-informed appreciation of the ethnic differences between women. Until the women's prison population is reduced, until more money is put into the prisons, and until there is a principled strategy for accommodating female differences of gender and ethnicity in a more judicious manner, it is difficult to expect any integrated system of management of the women's prisons to do much more than integrate and amplify the mistakes of the past.

As things stand at the present time, I see three possible scenarios for women's imprisonment in Britain in the future: (1) more-of-the-same-getting-worse-as-the-female prison-population-continues-to-grow. Let's call such a scenario *Women's Imprisonment Recycled*; (2) less-of-the-same-and-more-experimentation-with-progressive-projects-and-with-the-female-prison-population-fluctuating. Let's call that scenario

Women's Imprisonment Reformed; and finally, *Women's Imprisonment Reduced* – a closely regulated and holistic response to women's lawbreaking, with women's imprisonment, as we have known it, abolished. The first two scenarios will most probably alternate forever, unless there is a clear executive lead towards reduction.

Women' Imprisonment Recycled – forward to the Past

Unless someone with the requisite authority forces both sentencers and the Prison Service to reform their approaches to women's imprisonment the situation in the English women's prisons will rapidly get worse. Existing problems of overcrowding, management and regime conditions have already been detailed in this book, and most of them (together with others not mentioned here) have been thoroughly explicated in the Chief Inspector's Reports of the 1990s, the recommendations of which have, in the main, been ignored.

As we have already seen, at the end of 1997, the Chief Inspector of Prisons made 186 recommendations in relation to the Inspection of one prison alone. These recommendations, as well as making a number of criticisms specific to the Bullwood Hall site, also touched on most of the major issues which have been discussed in this book, and which are generalizable to all women's prisons in England, for example: the special needs of young female offenders; the need for consistency of rule interpretation between women's establishments; equal opportunities issues; and the possible adaptation of all kinds of security procedures to make them more relevant to the actual degree of risk posed by the female prisoner population.

Nonetheless, in addition to the catalogue of shortcomings listed by the Inspectors in report after report, there are also other worrying aspects of the continuing deterioration of the women's prison estate, regressive trends which will take a long time to reverse if they are not effectively addressed in the near future, and which, moreover, if allowed to continue unchecked, will effectively sabotage attempts at implementation of any of the reforms currently being canvassed. (See next section of this chapter for a discussion of some of the more radical of these proposed reforms).

Obviously, a continuing rise in the female prison population will make for more overcrowding, increased management problems and worsening conditions for both prisoners and staff. As, however, the question of sentencing reform will be discussed again below, in the section subtitled 'Women's imprisonment reduced' in the rest of this section I will concentrate on the adverse effects that the deteriorating conditions in women's prisons have had on staff morale. This is an issue that has been much neglected by the Prison Service, but it must be taken very seriously if progressive change is to occur within the women's establishments.

A major concern of many of the senior staff I spoke to, and also of some Board of Visitors, members was that present poor conditions in the prisons in general are provoking many of the better staff to leave the Service.

> All this legislation about home leave, security, searching, drugs – it's all negative and I think it disables individual officers. (BOV 1)

> There is enormous talent around. There are very good people, not only in terms of commitment, but in terms of knowledge, skill and expertise. But until the Service actually demonstrates that it's serious about moving in a forward direction, these people will remain frustrated. They will leave. The Service has already lost several really outstanding people in the last six months who have retired early because they have been seen as troublemakers, difficult people. (Senior Official in Home Office)

And if the good people leave, *and* conditions in the women's prisons get no better, young staff coming into the Service will have no measuring rod against which to chart declining standards and a spiral of ever-lower standards will set in. This was another concern of the Senior Official in the Home Office when I spoke with him:

> What is frightening is that you can see that in some establishments it [the lack of health and educational amenity caused by operational cuts] has actually eroded staff judgement, so that sometimes they can't actually see that what they are doing is wrong... The Prison Service gets away with locking up men for hours and days at a time, particularly when they're short of staff. And men tolerate it. In female establishments, particularly local prisons where you've got

the remand population for women, you can't do it. If you lock women up, they can't hack it – I know this is a generalization, but forget that for a moment – they can't hack it. They get very frustrated, worked up, violent, angry. If, on top of that you get a management that doesn't know what it is doing, it does what they do on the male side, and they lock-down. Once you do that you've increased the cycle and any vestiges of self-respect or self-esteem that the women had gets totally lost. They start damaging themselves or each other and that's the cycle that leads to carelessness. Then, what worries me is that the staff can become conditioned into not being able to recognize what any normal person would recognize as being part of any civilized approach. Once that starts, staff become anxious about confrontation with angry women and it's, 'Oh, we can't let them out'. And then they start not seeing that women not having clean clothing or that there are rats outside is relevant. It's a whole spiral, and it starts when the regime begins to be interrupted, and when staff are faced with a Prison Service that has no standards at all.

But this is a 'worst case scenario'. It is extremely unlikely that all the good staff will leave, and since the Inspectorate walked out of Holloway Prison in disgust at the dirty conditions there, prison staff seem to be much more conscious that the Inspectorate, at least, will not pull its punches when it comes to evaluating a prison's basic facilities. Most importantly, and as the Senior Official in the Home Office himself insisted, there are still a lot of very concerned and committed people working in the Service. Nonetheless, as officer after officer who was interviewed remarked, morale in 1997 was very low. Financial restrictions seemed to block all innovations. The strict security measures still in force meant that again and again, prison staff had to 'do good by stealth' (cf Carlen 1990).

> We're struggling for staff, and it really is stretching staff all the time, especially if you want to do quality work with them. (Prison Officer 2 – female)

> Things like incoming phone calls mean a lot to women, and I think that we're the only prison now that still run the incoming phone line – which means a tremendous lot to women. We just have to hide it when anyone from headquarters

comes round, because I think Michael Howard would pull the plugs out himself if he were here... (Governor No 4 and BOV 3 – talking to me together)

But even if the good staff stay in the Service, for how much longer can they be expected to 'do good by stealth' and against all the odds? In 1997, I still found a few officers expressing very punitive views about how prisoners should be treated, and a continuation in punitive cuts may unfortunately reinforce them in their views. Reforms in such a situation are likely to be uphill work, and there may even be an increase in punitiveness towards inmates if prison officers find that not only are they themselves being allowed fewer and fewer outlets for more positive work with prisoners but that, as a result of the negativism stemming from financial restrictions and punitive media interventions, they are having a much tougher, and more confrontational time on the landings and in the houses. As it was, even the most optimistic staff answered me very wearily when, at the end of their interviews, I asked them about the changes for good which they envisaged in the future – they obviously thought I had not understood how serious the financial cuts had been! An Education Officer neatly summed up what many other prison personnel had said:

If we're actually looking at where we're going in the future, then it's bleak. Unless the Government makes some changes, radical changes, and decides to put some more money into education, then education's going to suffer, as is the Probation Service. That is the big problem. Sorry. It's very much a matter of, 'Watch this space'. (Education Officer 2 – female)

There are other questions. If they do eventually go for a Director of Women, will that person have, not just responsibility, but *power*? (Probation Officer 8 – female)

Women's Imprisonment Reformed

A well-behaved woman convict with a sentence of five years or more may be permitted to spend the last nine months of her period of imprisonment in an 'approved refuge'. (Hobhouse and Brockway 1922:348)

A recurring theme in the talk of the prison personnel I interviewed was that women's prisons *could* be better. As is usual in most organizations and occupations, a very few staff harked back to a generalized golden past where *everything* had been better; more, however, referred to the short post-Woolf era, when the emphasis had been on humanity in the treatment of prisoners and Prison Department 'enablement' of staff in the performance of their duties (Woolf, 1991); all proffered ideas about ways in which the regimes could be made more constructive. Many of these ideas have been taken up in various official reports on the women's prisons, and I will not list all of them here. Suffice it to say that all reforms canvassed were predicated on assumptions that more money would have to be made available if prison regimes were to be boosted, that prison overcrowding would have to cease, and that certain categories of offender (eg the severely mentally disturbed) should not be held in prison conditions. The main types of reform mentioned ranged from the more traditional enhancement of regime activities, through the setting up of more specialized units, to a radical rethink of women's imprisonment which variously involved the setting up of hostels (to be run by the Prison Department) and halfway houses (to be run by other organizations acceptable to the courts).

When staff were asked about desirable changes in their own establishment the major items mentioned were: a greater emphasis on dynamic (rather than restrictive) security; more activities for prisoners – especially more paid work and educational activities; increased communication with families and other people outside prison; more imaginative and constructive ways of dealing with disruptive prisoners; and the employment of more specialist staff to provide both regime activities and specialist help to the many prisoners with a tangle of very complex problems.

Other changes were mentioned as being essentially related to the achievement of the primary objectives: high staff morale, pleasant prison environment, and a clear relationship between type of regime objectives and type of prisoner allocated. (This last was especially mentioned by staff of the open prisons who made the point that owing to the type of prisoner being sent to them (as a result of overcrowding), and also because of some of the security restrictions imposed post-Woodcock, they could no longer run what they considered to be an 'open' regime. As we have already seen, several prisoners concurred with this view, often arguing that the so-called 'open' prisons can be experienced as being more oppressive than the closed). What I personally found most heartening was that governors in particular tended to insist that the whole prison has to be conceived as a dynamic whole:

> I think that you've got to look after basics, and I think cleanliness is important in all prisons. Food also is important, quality of food. Then decor. I think that's very important because from the time we introduced pictures and colour schemes (allowing the Works Department to consult people and get colour schemes that were acceptable – ones that people felt comfortable with and proud of), people have taken care of the place. There's very little grafitti and, although 20 per cent of our prisoners are in for a crime of violence, in all the five or six years we have had pictures along the main corridor, we've only had one broken one. It adds to the ambience, the feel of the place. (Governor No 4 – male)

The same governor was also committed to founding what he called a 'Special Needs Unit':

> There are money constraints, but we shouldn't use that as an excuse. We've still got to carry on, and do what we can. It's maintaining the quality that is the thing. But I think that, in terms of development, what I would really like to see is a Special Needs Unit. You're familiar with Grendon aren't you? I mean, I don't want to turn [this prison] into a Grendon for females, but there is a crying need for – I call it a Special Needs Unit. Because it's about more than just drugs, or sex abuse – it's probably a mixture of both. It's about women who are lacking in confidence, seriously damaged, who don't need to be held in a closed prison, who are quite safe in the community, but who do need really skilled assistance with some of the problems they have here. That's why I would like to see a small residential unit set up which could have the services of psychologists and medical staff and probation-support staff, and with proper pogrammes to actually address their particular problems. You see, the problem with having dormitories is that if women do want to scream, shout and so

forth, it's very difficult in public. That is why we set up the Probation Service where we did. So that women could actually go down there, offload, and then, if they did cry, they could actually compose themselves before they came back to the house... Hopefully, when they leave here they should go out a little bit better in some areas, even if they've been damaged in some others. The danger is that you damage them more than you cure. (Governor No 4 – male)

Other types of specialist unit mentioned were for the mentally ill, very young offenders, women who had been sexually abused, women with children, and those serving exceptionally long sentences. What staff mentioned most frequently with approval, however, was the concept of the 'half-way house', some type of hostel-like establishment to which women could be sent half way through their sentences, and where relevant and feasible (in terms of children's schooling, for example), their babies and infant children could live with them. Such an arrangement would appear to provide, at one swoop, a satisfactory solution to the contradictory views on women's imprisonment that many of the staff had expressed, and to which there appeared to be no very satisfactory solution. The 'halfway house' idea would involve an element of retributive custody, but it would also recognize women's special needs and those of their children. A similar scheme (though not one involving a prior period of traditional prison custody) was put forward by NACRO after the Woolf Report (1991), and was discussed by Carlen and Tchaikowsky (1996) in the book *Prisons 2000* (Matthews and Francis 1996). I will now repeat those arguments, for not only are they still relevant, but they also illustrate why prison reform should never be piecemeal, and why, instead, it requires to be undertaken within a holistic and progressive programme of reduction (of the prison population) and (gender-tested) transformation (of prisons as we have known them).

Fear that the transforming objectives of radical critique will become neutralized if they are incorporated into the State's penal machinery in piecemeal fashion has always provoked ambivalence amongst prison reformers and theorists when they have been confronted with seemingly unequivocally-progressive proposals for prison reform. This is not because they are committed to forever grinding their penal axes: it is because prison reforms always take place within political conditions which might result in their outcomes being very different to the intentions of those who put the reforms in place. The concern about the fate of piecemeal reforms is threefold: first, that short-term reformist schemes often lend a spurious appearance of legitimacy to prison regimes without diminishing their fundamentally debilitating effects; second, that they will result in programmes which, though experienced positively by women already in prison, are seen by sentencers to provide justification for sending even more women to prison; and third, that they will involve innovations which, though they might *in principle* be radically progressive, are likely, *in practice,* either to be perverted by perversely punitive sentencing practices, or subverted by lack of adequate funding and support. Take, for example, the post-Woolf proposal by the government-funded National Association for the Care and Resettlement of Offenders (NACRO) that women prisoners should serve their sentences in 'community houses':

> In the long term the way to meet the vision of the Woolf Report would be to keep the small numbers of women in their home area, close to court, in houses set aside for the purpose. The women would reside there during custody and avail themselves of the community's services to supply the elements of their daily regime. This would be essential since it would be uneconomic for the Prison Service to provide full programmes in very small units. Contact with home and family would be maintained by proximity or by joint residence for young children, space permitting. (NACRO 1991:19)

This is an imaginative concept and could, in the best (Utopian) scenario, lead to the abolition of women's imprisonment as it is known at present (see the third possible future of women's imprisonment, described below). Yet once the proposal is assessed against the *backcloth of contemporary penal politics* in Britain, it is immediately apparent why women's prison-campaigners should carefully distinguish between the proposal's radical potential and the reformist, and even retrogressive, probabilities of its actual implementation. For in the context of The New Punitiveness, with its emphasis on young unmarried mothers as *the* folk-devils of late twentieth century 'welfare', it is very likely that the existence of such houses would soon be perceived by sentencers as providing yet another excuse to lock up more and more young women seen to be in need of 'training' as 'mothers'. Similarly, some of the proposal's rosier assumptions about women's need for family under all circumstances begin to fade when set against what is known about either domestic violence, or the non-existent 'family lives' of many young women prisoners who have been state-reared in local authority care. And finally, although the suggestion that, 'Allowing women in this situation to use community facilities would be essential' (NACRO 1991:19) is, in itself, an excellent one, it is appropriate to remind enthusiasts for 'community houses' that for the last twenty years (at least) it has been the constant complaint of workers attempting to deliver 'alternatives to custody' that their best efforts have been repeatedly subverted by the scarcity of *any* resources in the 'community' – and especially those most relevant to women's needs for example nursery schools, further education grants, satisfying work, move-on accommodation, crisis loans for furniture, and affordable care for elderly relatives – to name but a few. In short, if community houses for women prisoners were to be founded without stringent sentencing controls, and adequate funding and extensive community back-up facilities, they would soon deteriorate into *fin de siecle* workhouses for the welfare state's 'undeserving' and poverty-stricken mothers. Given the punitive nature of both government and courts at the end of the 1990s, attempted implementation of all the other reforms mentioned in this book could go the same (retrogressive) way – if not implemented as part of a holistic approach involving courts and social services.

So why continue to take seriously the proposal for community houses for women prisoners? For several reasons. First, because any *intention* to reduce the pains of imprisonment for women is *good in itself.* Secondly, because while prisons exist, in any form, such a good can only be pursued if campaigners continue to engage in democratic discussion and cooperative enterprise with prisoners, prison staff, prison administrators and opinion leaders. Thirdly, because it is essential to keep open to public view the inner workings of the whole carceral machinery; so that its endemic secrecy can be held in check, and its chronic tendency for periodic reversion from progressive to retrogressive practices constantly monitored.

The purpose of giving full recognition to the political conditions which *may* atrophy the radically progressive potential of new penal initiatives is *not* to enable campaigners to take refuge in a 'nothing works' nihilism. Instead, the *intention* in recognizing the contradictions between present realities and utopian desires is to facilitate analysis of the conditions in which present realities might begin to be otherwise. (For a much more optimistic view of the self-reforming potential in late 1990s British gaols by someone who has actually worked in them, see *Prisons of Promise* by Tessa West 1997.)

Women's Imprisonment Reduced

There is a total absence of co-ordination between elements of the criminal justice system, and until there is co-ordination, the issues that we have been talking about with regards to the Prison Service are not going to be addressed. Not until the Prison Service comes in from wherever it's poked itself for generations. (Senior Official in Home Office)

In typical Civil Service fashion there are different Departments that are looking at different bits of policy, and they all work in different ways. But the degree to which governors are consulted will depend on which Department is dealing with which bit of policy. (Governor No 5 – male) (See Prison Governors' Association 1995, for a succinct plea for a more co-ordinated criminal justice system)

The supporting arguments and evidence for the proposition that the female prison population should be reduced have already been detailed in the previous pages of this book. I will now, therefore, only briefly summarize the justifications for claiming yet again that there is an urgent need to reduce women's imprisonment: quantitatively, by curbing the excessive custodial sentencing of women presently being practised; qualitatively, by reducing the degree of imprisonment (of body and soul) experienced by women who continue to receive custodial sentences.

At the most fundamental and general level, there is no evidence that 'prison works' in terms of reducing the overall crime rate (see Tarling 1993). In relation to women in particular, statistical evidence suggests that the vast majority of females in prison are not a danger to the public (see Fletcher 1997). More qualitative research suggests that the social costs of keeping women in prison (in terms of the damage done to their families and, especially in the case of young girls, the women prisoners themselves) are enormous (see Eaton 1993:35–40; and Howard League 1997a).

Yet, as we have seen above, there is good reason to believe that in those serious cases where women are likely to continue to receive custodial sentences, the actual time served *could* be a less damaging experience if only there were far fewer women crowded into the prisons, and more places where they could be confined with dignity and in humane and women-wise establishments near to families or friends.

Nonetheless, and as I have argued elsewhere (Carlen 1990), a permanent quantitative reduction in the numbers of women held in custody will only be achieved as part of a holistic programme which limits the powers of the judiciary and the magistrates via a Sentencing Council one of whose many jobs might be to ensure that custodial sentences were normally being reserved for those women whose crimes had been so heinous that the rest of us should be protected from them; or, where that criterion had not been met, that sentencers had given grounds for the incarcerative sentence by referring to its appropriateness to the offender and the offence and also made very explicit exactly what they hoped to achieve by the custodial sentence awarded. However, while women's prisons exist, it is more than probable that they will be filled up. I therefore again make a plea that imprisonment should be abolished as a 'normal' punishment for women and that a maximum of only a hundred places should be retained for female offenders convicted or accused of abnormally serious crimes. During that time:

1. Women convicted or accused of abnormally serious crimes should only be imprisoned after their cases have been referred by the trial judge to a Sentencing Council who would make the final adjudication.
2. There should be close monitoring of the sentencing of all women and especially of those whose sentences run counter to the usual tariff.
3. A fundamental and far-reaching examination of *all* sentencing should be undertaken as called for by Andrew Ashworth (1988).

4. The regimes, environments and sentence plans developed for the women who continue to receive custodial sentences should be entirely different to those presently in force.
5. The present staff of the women's prisons should be fully involved in the development of more imaginative regimes, environments and sentence plans.
6. The Prison Department should appoint a Director of Women's Penal Confinement.
7. An Independent Women and Penal Confinement Unit should be founded to monitor developments within women's establishments and to ensure the gender-testing of all regime innovations.

When in 1990 I proposed that imprisonment should be abolished as the usual punishment for offences committed by women (and, incidentally gave a much more detailed justification than I have given here – see Carlen 1990:117–25) the proposal was greeted with a certain amount of scepticism, with one prominent radio interviewer asking (tongue in cheek) whether the implementation of such a plan would be an invitation to (male) burglars to retire knowing that their wives or girlfriends could carry on the business with impunity. Since then, however, there has been much more support for the inception of very different types of penal confinement for women (see Woolf 1991; HM Chief Inspector of Prisons 1997b; also Chapman 1996; Hayman 1996 for a comparative study of practice in England and Holland). Talk of halfway houses, 'transitional prisons' and community prisons is now commonplace, with, in some instances, enthusiasts even suggesting that radical change in the women's sector could be an experimental forerunner to some more constructive approaches in the men's:

> What we want is smaller, open prisons in the community, and in an urban context – that's what we want for women. I think they could also be very good forerunners for men as well. (Senior Official in Home Office)

And why not? But unless there is adequate support from government, social services and the rest of the criminal justice system – in other words, unless there is a holistic approach – all these imaginative schemes will not even be successfully implemented for *women*. Women's imprisonment will not be reduced.

The routine imprisonment of women for less serious crimes will not be abolished. The rarer imprisonment of women for very serious crimes will not be transformed into the even rarer (but more womenwise) women's penal confinement. And the present waste of women's imprisonment will continue, with alternating periods of reform and regression, and always with a demoralized workforce.

The main argument of this book is that women's imprisonment could be both otherwise and womenwise; and all the evidence adduced from a variety of prison personnel indicate that the requisite skills, commitment and imaginative creativity are already available to make it so. As the millennium approaches, therefore, let us hope that well before the dawn of the new century we will see the demise of this twentieth century's sledgehammer of a system of women's imprisonment; and that, in its place, we will witness the birth of a more holistic, womenwise response to girls and women in criminal trouble.

References

Abernethy, R. and Hammond, N. (1996) 'Working with Foreign Offenders: A Role for The Probation Service' in P. Green (ed.) *Drug Couriers: A New Perspective*, London, 8 Quartet Books, pp. 136–50.

Adelberg, E. and Currie, C. (eds) (1987) *Too Few To Count*, Vancouver, Press Gang.

Adler, Z. (1987) *Rape On Trial*, London, Routledge and Kegan Paul.

Allen, H. (1987) *Justice Unbalanced*, Buckingham, Open University Press.

Ashworth, A. (1988) 'The Road to Sentencing Reform' in *Prison Reform No 5*, London, Prison Reform Trust.

Aungles, A. (1994) *The Prison and The Home*, Sydney, Institute of Criminology.

Bain, K. and Parker, H. (1997) *Drinking With Design: Alcopops, Designer Drinks and Youth Drugs Cultures*, London, Portman Group.

Barclay, P. (1995) *Joseph Rowntree Inquiry into Income and Wealth*, Vol. 1, York, Joseph Rowntree Foundation.

Bardsley, B. (1987) *Flowers in Hell: An Investigation into Women in Crime*, London, Pandora.

Bienek, H. (1972) *The Cell*, Santa Barbara, Unicorn Press.

Blair, T. (1993) 'Perrie Lecture March 1993 – The Future of the Prison Service' in J. Reynolds and U. Smartt (eds) *Prison Policy and Practice*, Leyhill, Prison Service Journal.

Boyle, C. *et al.* (1985) *A Feminist Review of Criminal Law*, Canada, Minister of Supply and Services.

Brittan, A. (1989) *Masculinity and Power*, Oxford, Blackwell.

Bull, D. and Wilding, P. (eds) (1983) *Thatcherism and The Poor*, London, Child Poverty Action Group.

Byrne, D. (1987) 'Rich and Poor: The Growing Divide' in A. Walker and C. Walker (eds) *The Growing Divide: A Social Audit*, London, Child Poverty Action Group.

Carlen, P. (1983) *Women's Imprisonment*, London, Routledge and Kegan Paul.

Carlen, P. (1986) 'Psychiatry in Prisons: Promises, Premises, Practices and Politics', in P. Miller and N. Rose (eds) *The Power of Psychiatry*, Cambridge, Polity Press.

Carlen P. (1987) 'Out of Care and into Custody' in P. Carlen and A. Worrall (eds) *Gender, Crime and Justice*, Buckingham, Open University Press.

Carlen, P. (1988) *Women, Crime and Poverty*, Buckingham, Open University Press.

Carlen, P. (1990) *Alternatives To Women's Imprisonment*, Buckingham, Open University Press.

Carlen, P. (1994) 'Why Study Women's Imprisonment? Or Anyone Else's?' in Roy King and Mike Maguire (eds) *Prison In Context* Oxford, Clarendon Press.

Carlen, P. (1995) 'Virginia, Criminology, and The Anti-Social Control of Women' in T. Blumberg and S. Cohen (eds) *Punishment and Social Control*, New York, Aldine de Gruyter

Carlen, P. (1996) *Jigsaw – A Political Criminology of Youth Homelessness*, Buckingham, Open University Press.

Carlen P., Christina, D., Hicks, J., O'Dwyer, J. and Tchaikovsky, C. (1985) *Criminal Women*, Cambridge, Polity Press.

Carlen, P. and Tchaikovsky, C. (1996) 'Women's Imprisonment at the End of the Twentieth Century' in P. Francis and R. Matthews, (eds) *Prisons 2000*, London, Macmillan.

Carlen, P. and Wardhaugh, J. (1991) 'Locking Up Our Daughters' in P. Carter, T. Jeffs, and K. Smith (eds) *Social Work and Social Welfare Yearbook 3*, Buckingham, Open University Press

Carlen, P. and Worrall, A. (1987) *Gender, Crime and Justice*, Buckingham, Open University Press.

Carrington, K. (1993) *Offending Girls: Sex, Youth and Justice*, Sydney, Allen and Unwin.

Catan, L. (1988) *The Development of Young Children in HMP Mothers and Baby Units*, Working Papers in Psychology, No. 1, University of Sussex.

Catan, L. (1992) 'Infants with Mothers in Prison', in R. Shaw, *Prisoners' Children*, London, Routledge.

Cavadino, P. (1997) 'Pre-Sentence Reports: The Effects of Legislation and National Standards' in *British Journal Of Criminology*, Vol. 37, No. 4 Autumn.

Chapman, J. (1996) *Community Homes for Women Prisoners*, Replay Trust. Thame, Oxon.

Cheney, D. (1993) *Into the Dark Tunnel: Foreign Prisoners in the British Prison System*, London, Prison Reform Trust.

Chesler, P. (1974) *Women and Madness*, London, Allen Lane.

Chiquada, R. (1997) *Black Women's Experiences of Criminal Justice: A Discourse on Disadvantage*, Sussex, Waterside Press.

Clare, A. and Thompson, J. (1985) *Report Made on Visits to C1 Unit, Holloway Prison*, London, National Council for Civil Liberties.

Clayton, M. (1996, first published 1988) 'Equal Opportunities in the Prison Service' in J. Reynolds and U. Smartt (1996) *Prison Policy and Practice*, Leyhill, Prison Service Journal, pp. 199–206.

Cohen, S. and Taylor, L. (1972) *Psychological Survival*, Harmondsworth, Penguin.

Cohen, S. and Taylor, L. (1978) *Prison Secrets*, London, RAP and NCCL

Cook, D. (1988) *Rich Law, Poor Law*, Buckingham, Open University Press.

Coote, A. and Campbell, B. (1987) *Sweet Freedom*, 2nd edition, Oxford, Basil Blackwell.

Cousins, M. (1980) 'Mens Rea: A Note on Sexual Difference, Criminology and the Law', in P. Carlen and M. Collison (eds) *Radical Issues in Criminology*, Oxford, Martin Robertson.

Coward, R. (1984) *Female Desire*, London, Paladin

Currie, E. (1996) *Is America Really Winning the War on Crime and Should Britain Follow Its Example?* London, NACRO.

Dahl, T. S. (1987) *Women's Law: An Introduction to Feminist Jurisprudence*, Oslo, Norwegian University Press.

Daly, K. (1994) *Gender, Crime and Punishment*, New Haven and London, Harvard University Press.

Davies, I. (1990) *Writers in Prison*, Oxford, Blackwell.

Davies, M. (1974) *Prisoners of Society*, London, Routledge.

Dennis, N. and Erdos, G. (1992) *Families Without Fatherhood*, London, IEA Health and Welfare Unit.

Department of Health (1992) *Inspection of Facilities for Mothers and Babies in Prison*, London, Department of Health.

Devlin, A. (1998) *Invisible Women*, Sussex, Waterside Press.

Dobash, R. and Dobash, R. (1979) *Violence Against Wives*, London, Open Books.

Dobash, R., Dobash, R. and Gutteridge, S. (1986) *The Imprisonment of Women*, Oxford, Blackwell.

Dockley, A. (1996) 'Yet another male policy ... in *Criminal Justice*, Vol. 14, No. 3 London, Howard League.

Dominelli, L. (1984) 'Differential Justice: Domestic Labour, Community Service and Female Offenders', *Probation Journal*, 3(3), 100–3.

Donzelot, J. (1979) *The Policing of Families*, London, Hutchinson.

Dumas, A. (1986) *La Dame Aux Caméllias*, Oxford, Penguin.

Durkheim, E. (1964) *Rules of Sociological Method*, New York, Macmillan.

Dworkin, A. (1981) *Pornography: Men Possessing Women*, London, Women's Press.

Eaton, M. (1986) *Justice for Women: Family, Court and Social Control*, Buckingham, Open University Press.

Eaton, M. (1993) *Women After Prison*, Buckingham, Open University Press.

Edwards, S. (1984) *Women on Trial*, Manchester, Manchester University Press.

Ehrenreich, B. and English, D. (1979) *For Her Own Good*, London, Pluto Press.

Eichenbaum, L. and Orbach, S. (1983) *What Do Women Want?* London, Michael Joseph.

Farrington, D. and Morris, A. (1983) 'Sex, Sentencing and Conviction' *Journal of Criminology*, 23(3), July, 229–48.

Feeley, M. and Little, D. (1991) 'The Vanishing Female: The Decline of Women in the Criminal Process, 1687–1912', *Law and Society Review*, Vol. 25, No. 4.

Fineman, M. and Thomadsen, N. (eds) (1991) *At the Boundaries of Law*, New York, Routledge.

Fishman, L. (1990) *Women at the Wall*, New York, State University of New York Press.

Fletcher, H. (1997) *Women and Crime*, London National Association of Probation Officers.

Foucault, M. (1977) *Discipline and Punish: The Birth of the Prison*, London, Allen and Unwin.

Giddens, A. (1992) *Human Societies*, Cambridge, Polity Press.

Giddens, A. (1997) *Sociology: Introductory Readings*, Cambridge, Polity Press.

Gibbens, T. C. N. (1971) 'Female Offenders', *British Journal of Hospital Medicine*, September.

Glendinning, C. and Millar, J. (eds) (1988) *Women and Poverty in Britain*, Brighton, Wheatsheaf.

Glendinning, C. and Millar, J. (eds) (1992) *Women and Poverty in Britain: The 1990s*, Brighton, Harvester, Wheatsheaf.

Goffman, E. (1968) *Asylums*, Harmondsworth, Penguin.

Grbich, J. (1991) 'The Body in Legal Theory' in M. A. Fineman and N. S. Thomadsen (eds) (1991) *At the Boundaries of Law*, New York, Routledge, pp. 61–76.

Green, P. (1996) 'Drug Couriers: The Construction of a Public Enemy', in P. Green (ed.) *Drug Couriers: A New Perspective*, London, Quartet Books, pp. 1–20.

Green, P. (ed.) (1996) *Drug Couriers: A New Perspective*, London, Quartet Books.

Hagell, A., Newburn, T. and Rowlingson, K. (1995) *Financial Difficulties on Release from Prison*, London, Police Studies Institute.

Hale, C. (1998) 'Ecologies of Crime' in P. Carlen and R. Morgan (eds) *Crime Unlimited? Questions For The Twentieth Century*, London, Macmillan.

Hall, S., Critcher, C., Jefferson, T., Clarke, J. and Roberts, B. (1978) *Policing the Crisis*, London, Macmillan.

Hayman, S. (1996) *Community Prisons For Women*, London, Prison Reform Trust.

Heaven, O. (1996) 'Hibiscus: Working with Nigerian Women Prisoners', in P. Green (ed.) *Drug Couriers: A New Perspective*, London, Quartet Books.

Hedderman, C. and Gelsthorpe, L. (1997) *Understanding the Sentencing of Women*, Home Office Research Study 170, London, HMSO.

Heidensohn, F. (1985) *Women and Crime*, London, Macmillan.

Hobhouse, S. and A. Fenner Brockway (eds) (1922) *English Prisons Today: Being the Report of the Prison System Enquiry Committee*, London, Longmans.

HM Chief Inspector of Prisons (1997a) *HM Prison Holloway: Report Of An Unannounced Inspection*, London, Home Office.

HM Chief Inspector of Prisons (1997b) *Women in Prison: A Thematic Review*, London, Home Office.

HM Chief Inspector of Prisons (1997c) *HM Young Offender Institution BULL-WOOD HALL Part A Executive Summary* London, Home Office.

HM Chief Inspector of Prisons (1997d) *HM Young Offender Institution BULL-WOOD HALL Part B Main Report*, London, Home Office.

HM Inspectorate of Probation (1991) *Report on Women Offenders and Probation Service Provision*, London, Home Office, July.

HM Prisons Inspectorate (1993) *HMP Durham*, London, Home Office.

HM Prisons Inspectorate (1994) *HMP Bullwood Hall*, London, Home Office.

HM Prisons Inspectorate (1996) *HMP Durham*, London, Home Office.

HM Prison Service (1996a) *Equal Opportunities in the Prison Service*, London HM Prison Service Personnel Directorate.

HM Prison Service (1996b) *Drug Misuse in Prison*, London, Home Office.

Home Office (1970) *Treatment of Women and Girls in Custody*, London.

Home Office (1982) *Prison Statistics for England and Wales 1981*, CMND 8654, London.

Home Office (1985) *HM Prison Holloway*, Report by Chief Inspector of Prisons, London, Home Office.

Home Office (1988) *Punishment, Custody and the Community*, CM424, London, HMSO.

Home Office (1992a) *The National Prison Survey, 1991: Main Findings*, Home Office Research Study 128, London, HMSO.

Home Office (1992b) *Gender and the Criminal Justice System*, London, Home Office.

Home Office (1994) *The Escape from Whitemoor Prison on Friday September 9th September 1994* (The Woodcock Enquiry) CM 2741, London, HMSO.

Home Office (1995a) *Prison Statistics England and Wales 1993*, CM 2893, London, Home Office.

Home Office (1995b) *Review of Prison Service Security in England and Wales and the Escape from Parkhurst Prison on Tuesday 3rd January* (The Learmont Inquiry), London, HMSO, CM 3020.

Home Office (1995c) *Race and Criminal Justice System 1995*, Croydon, Home Office and Statistics Directorate.

Home Office (1996a) *The Prison Population in 1995*, Issue 14/96 London, Home Office.

Home Office (1996b) *Prison Statistics in England and Wales 1995* CM 3355, London, HMSO.

Home Office (1996c) *British Crime Survey*, London, HMSO.

Home Office (1997a) *Projections of Long Term Trends in the Prison Population to 2005*, Home Office Statisitcal Bulletin Issue 7/97.

Home Office (1997b) *The Prison Population in 1996*, Home Office Statistical Bulletin 18/97, July, London, Home Office.

Howard League (1993) *The Voice of a Child*, London, Howard League.

Howard League (1994) *Families Matter*, London, Howard League.

Howard League (1996) *Prison Mother and Baby Units*, London, Howard League Information.

Howard League (1997a) *Lost Inside: The Imprisonment of Teenage Girls*, London, Howard League.

Howard League (1997b) *The Prison Population in 1996*, London Howard League.

Howe, A. (1994) *Punish and Critique: Towards a Feminist Analysis of Penality*, London, Routledge.

Hudson, B. (1984) 'Femininity and Adolescence' in A. McRobbie and M. Nava (eds) *Gender and Generation*, London, Macmillan.

Hutter, B. and Williams, G. (1981) *Controlling Women*, London, Croom Helm.

Iles, C. (1986) *Patriarchal Therapeutism*, PhD thesis, Kent University, England.

Jones, S. (1997) *Incentives and Earned Research: An Overview*, London, HM Prison Service.

Kennedy, H. (1992) *Eve Was Framed*, London, Chatto and Windus.

Laffargue, B. and Godefroy, T. (1989) 'Economic Cycles and Punishment: Unemployment and Imprisonmnent. A Time Series Study: France 1920–1985', *Contemporary Crises*, 13:371–404.

Lester, A. and Taylor, P. (1989) *'H' Wing, HM Prison, Durham*, London, Women in Prison.

Liebling, A. (1992) *Suicides in Prison*, London, Routledge.

Liebling, A. and Muir, M. (1997) 'IEP: National Evaluation Research', *Prison Research and Development Bulletin*, Vol. 3, February 1997, London, HM Prison Service.

Lewis, D. (1997) *Hidden Agendas: Politics, Law and Disorder*, London, Hamish Hamilton.

Loader, I. (1996) *Youth, Policing and Democracy*, London, Macmillan.

MacKinnon, C. (1987) 'Feminism, Marxism, Method and the State: Toward Feminist Jurisprudence', in S. Harding, *Feminism and Methodology*, Buckingham, Open University Press.

Maden, A., Swinton, M. and Gunn, J. (1994) 'A Criminological and Psychiatric Survey of Women Serving A Prison Sentence' *British Journal of Criminology*, Vol. 34, No. 2.

Mandaraka-Sheppard, A. (1986) *The Dynamics of Aggression in Women's Prisons in England*, London, Gower.

Matthews, R. and Francis, P. (eds) (1996) *Prisons 2000*, London, Macmillan.

Maybrick, Mrs F. E. (1905) *Mrs Maybrick's Own Story – My Fifteen Lost Years*, New York and London, Funk and Wagnell.

McConville, S. (1995) 'The Victorian Prison', in N. Morris and D. Rothman (eds) *The Oxford History Of The Prison*, Oxford, Oxford University Press.

McRobbie, A. (1991) *Feminism and Youth Culture*, London, Macmillan.

McShane, Y. (1980) *Daughter of Evil*, London, W. H. Allen.

Melossi, D. and Paverini, M. (1981) *The Prison and the Factory*, London, Macmillan.

Messerschmidt, J. (1986) *Capitalism, Patriarchy and Crime*, Totowa, NJ, Rowan and Littlefield

Meyer, P. (1977) *The Child and the State*, Cambridge, Cambridge University Press.

Morgan, R. and Carlen, P. (1998) 'Regulating Crime Control', in P. Carlen and R. Morgan (eds) *Crime Unlimited?* London, Macmillan.

Morris, A., Wilkinson, C. Tisi, A. and others (1995) *Managing the Needs of Female Prisoners*, London, Home Office.

Murray, C. (1984) *Losing Ground: American Social Policy 1950–1980*, New York, Basic Books.

Murray, C. (1990) *The Emerging British Underclass*, London, Institute of Economic Affairs.

NACRO (1985) *Mothers and Babies in Prison*, London, NACRO.

NACRO (1991) *A Fresh Start for Women Prisoners*, London, NACRO.

NAPO (1988) *Punishment, Custody and Community: The Response of the National Association of Probation Officers*, London NAPO.

O'Dwyer, J and Carlen, P. (1985) 'Surviving Holloway and Other Women's Prisons' in P. Carlen *et al.*, *Criminal Women*, Cambridge, Polity Press.

O'Dwyer, J., Wilson J. and Carlen, P. (1987) 'Women's Imprisonment in England, Wales and Scotland' in P. Carlen and A. Worrall (eds) (1987) *Gender, Crime and Justice*, Buckingham, Open University Press.

Open University (1989) *Social Sciences: Crime, Justice and Society: Supplementary Offprints Booklet, Block A*, Milton Keynes, Open University.

Ostfeld, A., Kasl, S., D'Atri, D. and Fitzgerald, E. (1987) *Stress, Crowding and Blood Pressure in Prison*, Hillsdale, NJ, Lawrence Erlbaum Associates.

Padell, U. and Stevenson, P. (1988) *Insiders*, London, Virago.

Peckham, A. (1985) *A Woman in Custody*, London, Fontana.

Penal Affairs Consortium (1996) *The Imprisonment of Women: Some Facts and Figures*, 169, Clapham Rd, London, SW9 OPU.

Pitman, D. and Gordon, C. (1958) *Revolving Door*, Illinois, Free Press.

Polity (1994) *The Polity Reader in Gender Studies*, pp. 305–309, Polity Press, Cambridge.

Priestley, P. (1985) *Victorian Prison Lives*, London, Methuen.

Priestley, P. (1995) *Jail Journeys*, London, Routledge.

Prison Governors Association (1995) *A Manifesto for Change*, Prison Governors Association.

Prison Reform Trust (1993) *Does Prison Work?* London, Prison Reform Trust.

Prison Reform Trust (1996) *Women in Prison: Recent Trends and Developments*, London, Prison Reform Trust.

Prison Service Security Group (1996) *Mandatory Drug Testing*, London, Home Office.

Radford, J. and Russell, D. (1992) (eds) *Femicide*, Buckingham, Open University Press.

Redcar, R. (1990) (ed.) *Dissenting Opinions*, Sydney, Allen and Unwin.

Reynolds, J. and Smartt, U. (eds) (1996) *Prison Policy and Practice*, Leyhill, Prison Service Journal.

Rock, P. (1995) *Reconstructing A Women's Prison*, Oxford, Oxford University Press.

Rose, N. (1989) *Governing the Soul*, London, Routledge.

Rutherford, A. (1996) *Transforming Criminal Policy*, Winchester, Waterside Press.

Sachs, A. and Wilson, J. (1978) *Sexism and the Law*, Oxford, Martin Robertson.

Seear, N. and Player, E. (1986) *Women in the Penal System*, London, Howard League.

Shaw, R. (1992) *Prisoners' Children: What are the Issues?* London, Routledge.

Sim, J. (1990) *Medical Power in Prisons*, Buckingham, Open University Press.

Smart, C. (1989) *Feminism and the Power of Law*, London, Routledge.

Smart, C. (1992) (ed.) *Regulating Womanhood*, London, Routledge.

Smith, A. (1962) *Women in Prison*, London, Stevens.

Sparks, R. (1995) 'The Barlinnie Unit: An Obituary', *Prison Writing*, No. 6, pp. 76–81.

Stanley, A. (1996) 'Deportation and Drug Couriers' in P. Green (ed.) *Drug Couriers: A New Perspective*, London, Quartet Books, pp. 112–126.

Swift, S. (1996) 'Women and Prison', *Prison Service Journal*, March, No. 10.

Tarling, R. (1993) *Analysing Offending Data*, London, HMSO.

Women's National Commission (1991) *Women and Prison*, London, Cabinet Office.

West, T. (1997) *Prisons of Promise*, Winchester, Waterside Press.

Wilson, E. (1977) *Women and the Welfare State*, London, Tavistock.

Woolf (1991) Report of an Inquiry by Lord Justice Woolf and His Honour Judge Stephen Tumin, *Prison Disturbances April 1990*, CMND 1456, London, HMSO.

Woolf, V. (1986, first published 1938) *Three Guineas*, London, Hogarth Press.

Worrall, A. (1981) 'Out of Place: Female Offenders in Court', *Probation Journal*, 28(3) pp. 90–93.

Worrall, A. (1990) *Offending Women*, London, Routledge.

Worrall, A. (1997) *Punishment in the Community*, London, Longman.

Zedner, L. (1991) *Women, Crime and Custody in Victorian England*, Oxford, Clarendon Press.

Index